My Life Beyond
AUTISM

A Mayo Clinic patient story
by Hey Gee and C. Ano

Foreword

Hi there, my name is C. Ano and I'm autistic. I didn't come to the full realization that I had autism until I was 10 years old, but even then I felt like I didn't fit in and wasn't really living a normal life.

Just like Tracy in this book, I like to put some toys in front of a cardboard green screen and make movies with them. I also like to draw, watch videos on YouTube and play Robot with my brother. (He came up with the game and I just joined in.) If your teacher is reading this in the classroom, you are parents who just found out your child has autism, you are friends of mine, or you are anyone else, I hope you like this book.

C. Ano

"

I JUST WANT TO BE TREATED LIKE EVERYONE ELSE

"

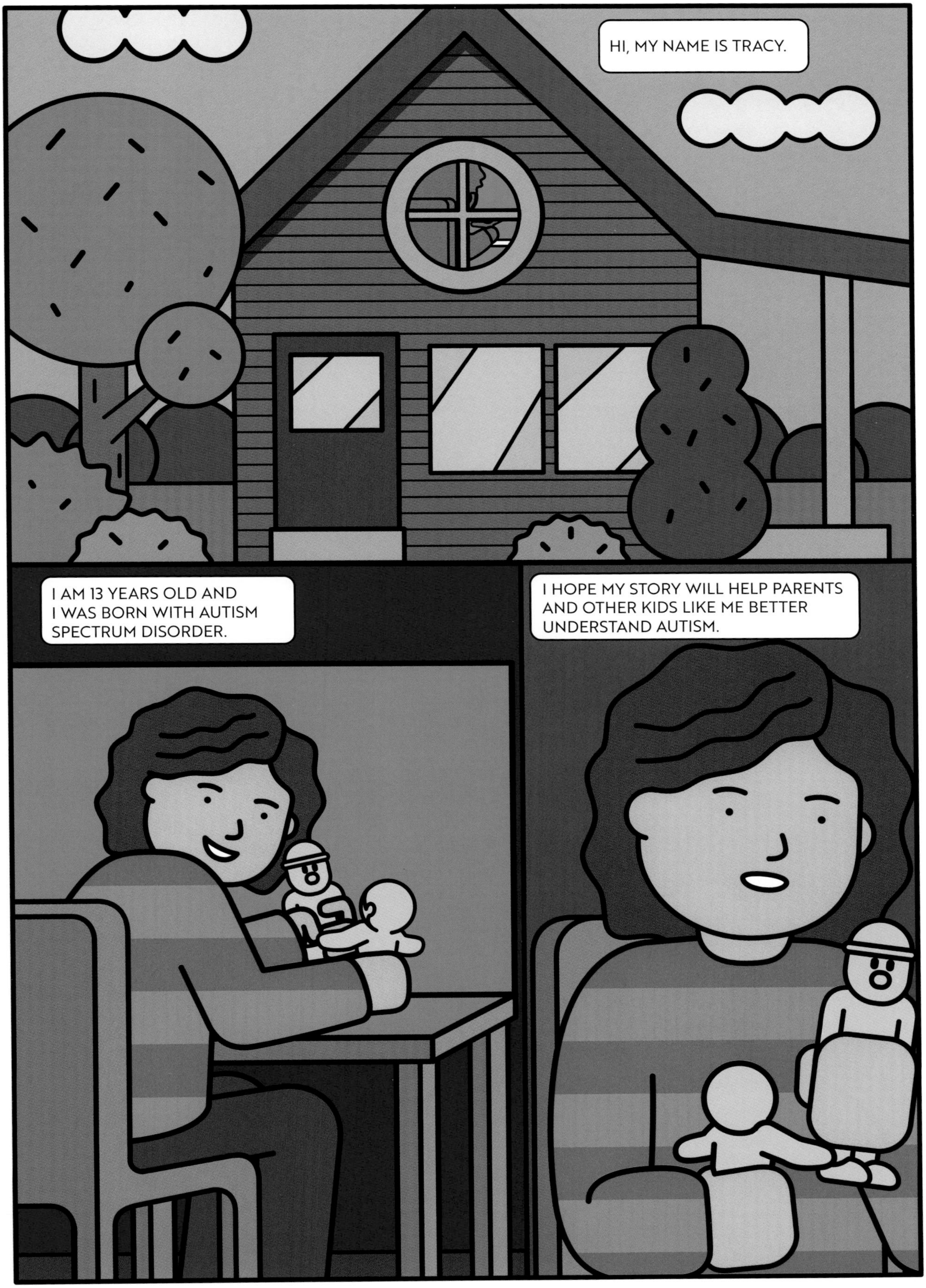
HI, MY NAME IS TRACY.
I AM 13 YEARS OLD AND I WAS BORN WITH AUTISM SPECTRUM DISORDER.
I HOPE MY STORY WILL HELP PARENTS AND OTHER KIDS LIKE ME BETTER UNDERSTAND AUTISM.

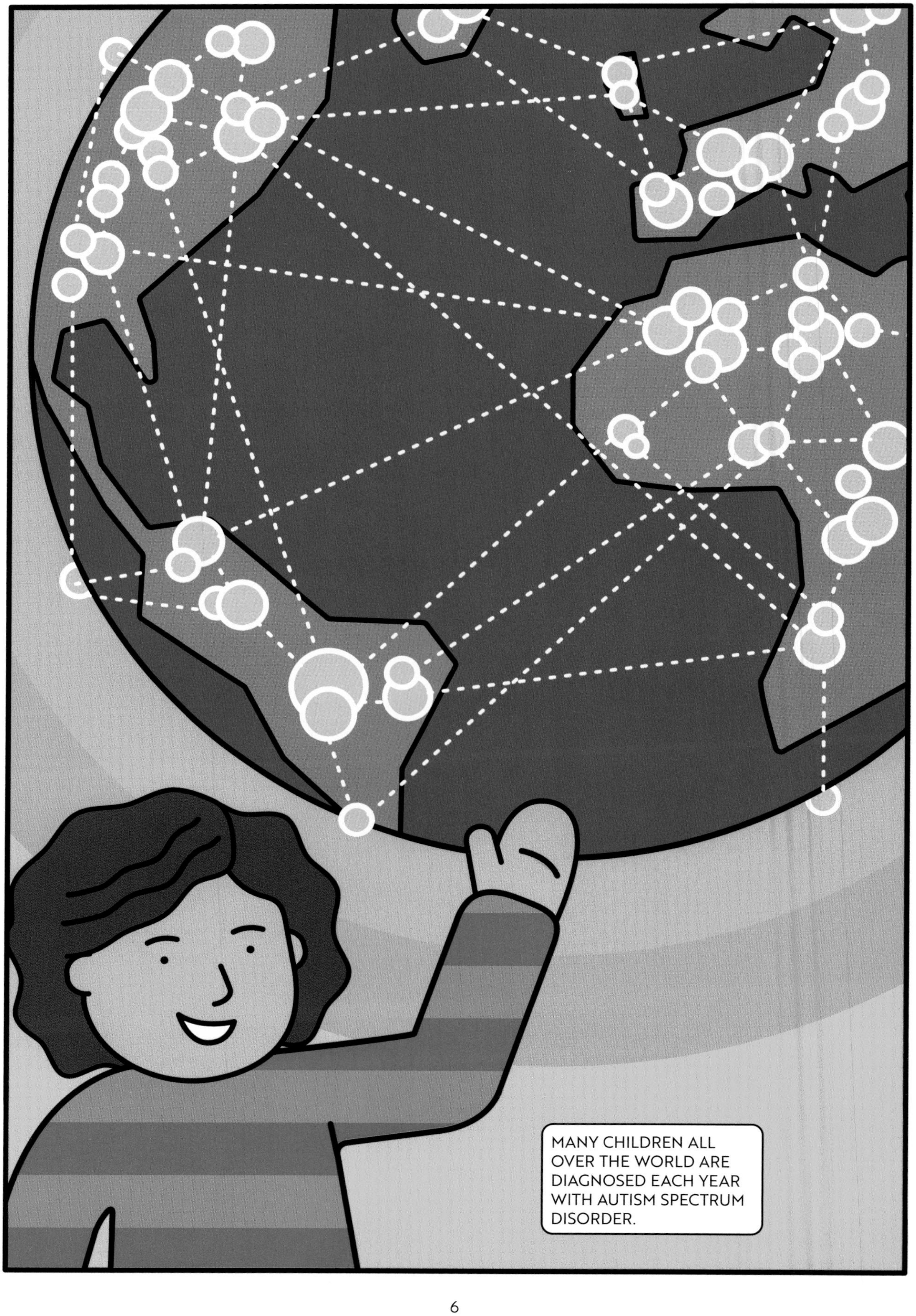
MANY CHILDREN ALL OVER THE WORLD ARE DIAGNOSED EACH YEAR WITH AUTISM SPECTRUM DISORDER.

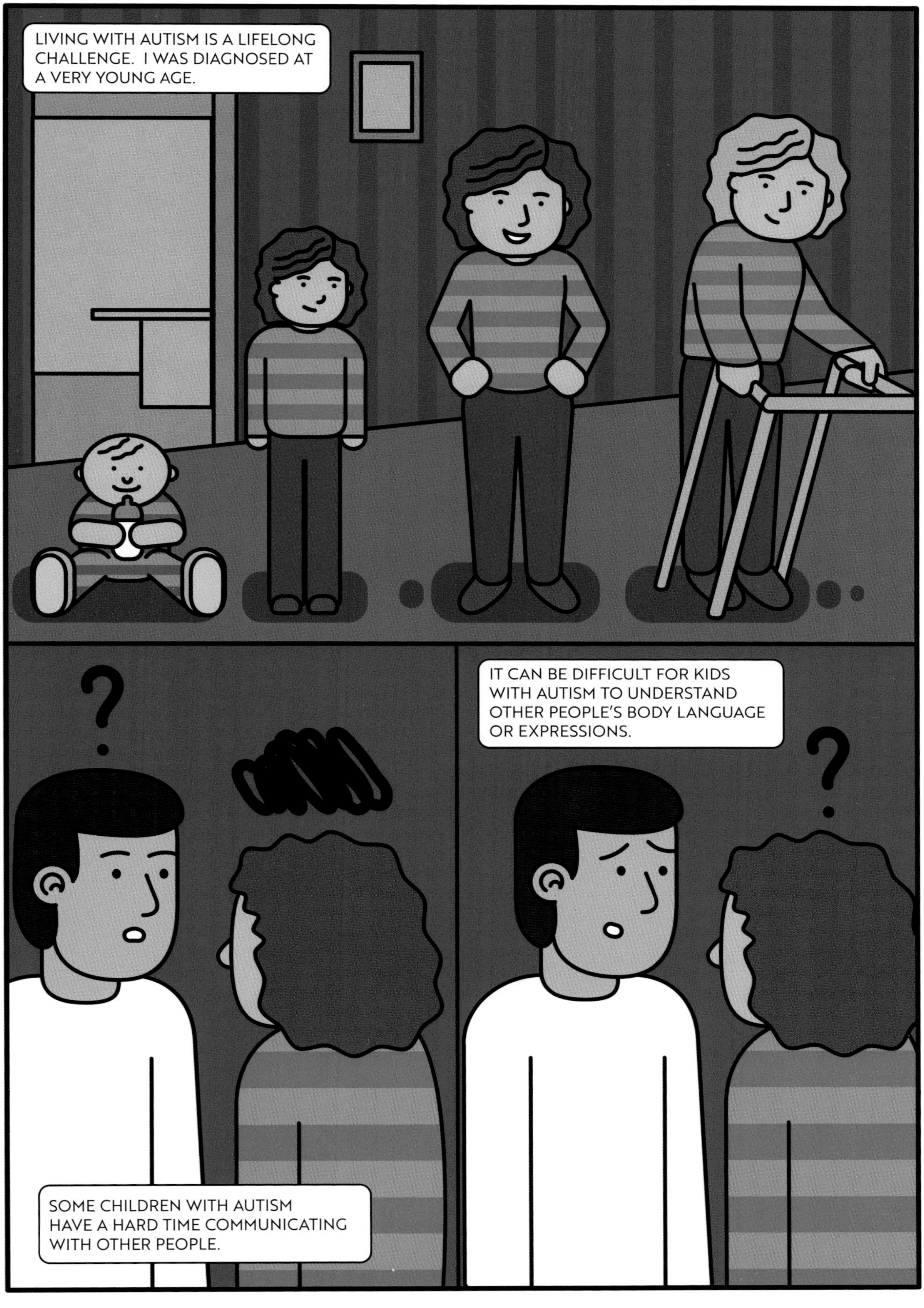
LIVING WITH AUTISM IS A LIFELONG CHALLENGE. I WAS DIAGNOSED AT A VERY YOUNG AGE.
?
SOME CHILDREN WITH AUTISM HAVE A HARD TIME COMMUNICATING WITH OTHER PEOPLE.
IT CAN BE DIFFICULT FOR KIDS WITH AUTISM TO UNDERSTAND OTHER PEOPLE'S BODY LANGUAGE OR EXPRESSIONS.
?

CHILDREN WITH AUTISM CAN TAKE LONGER TO UNDERSTAND INFORMATION.

SOMETIMES WE REPEAT WHAT WE DO, SAY OR THINK OVER AND OVER AND OVER.

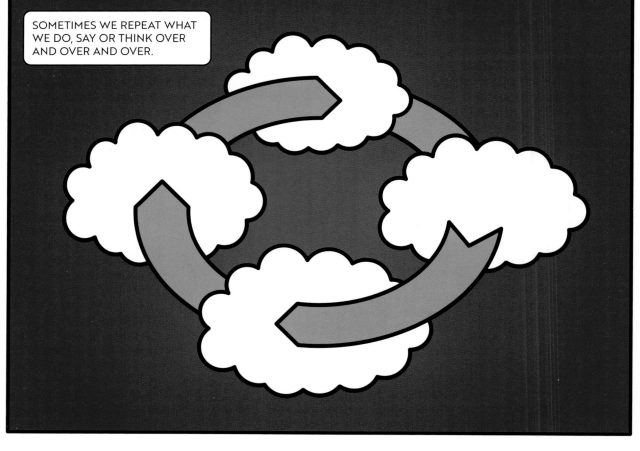

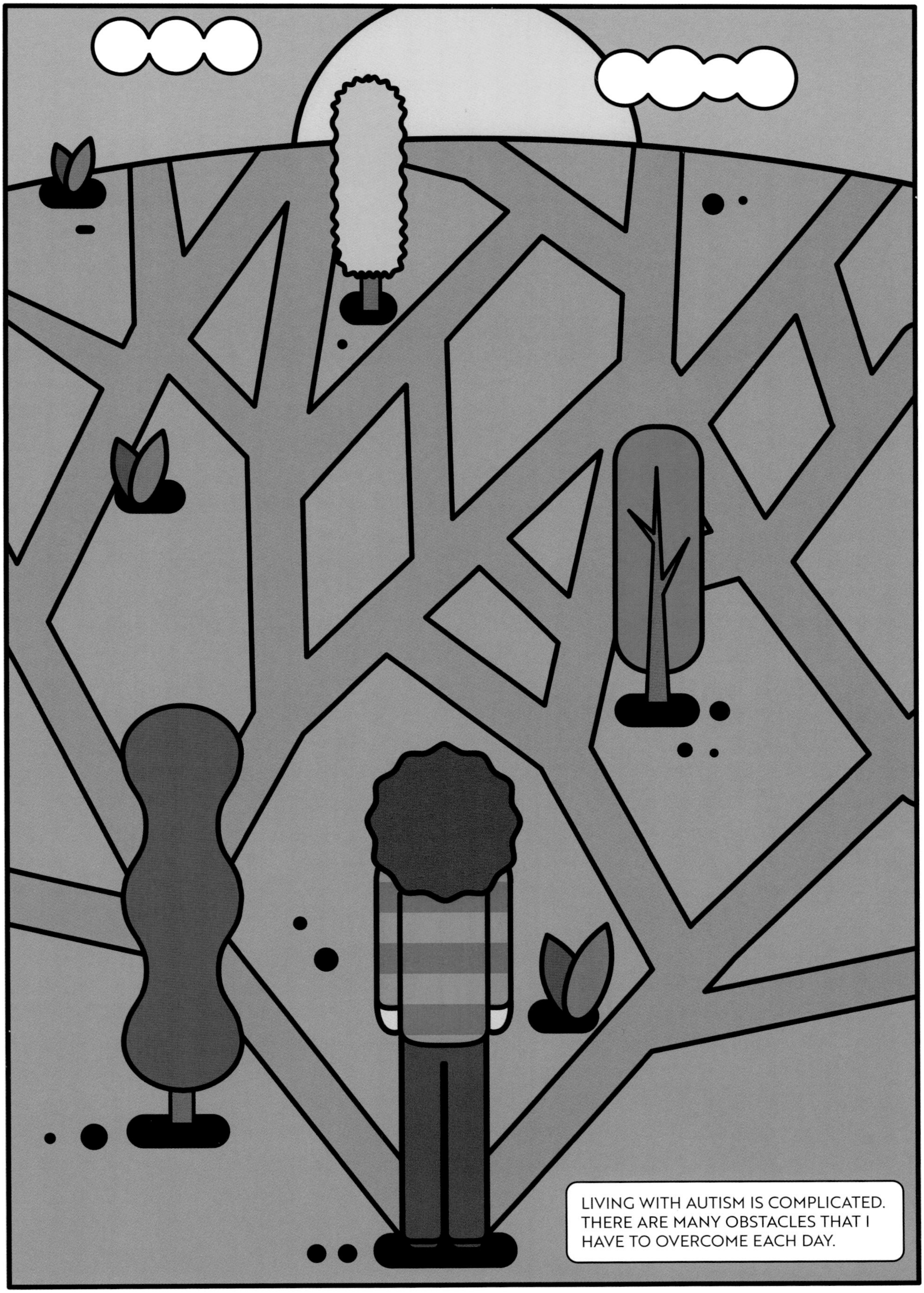
LIVING WITH AUTISM IS COMPLICATED. THERE ARE MANY OBSTACLES THAT I HAVE TO OVERCOME EACH DAY.

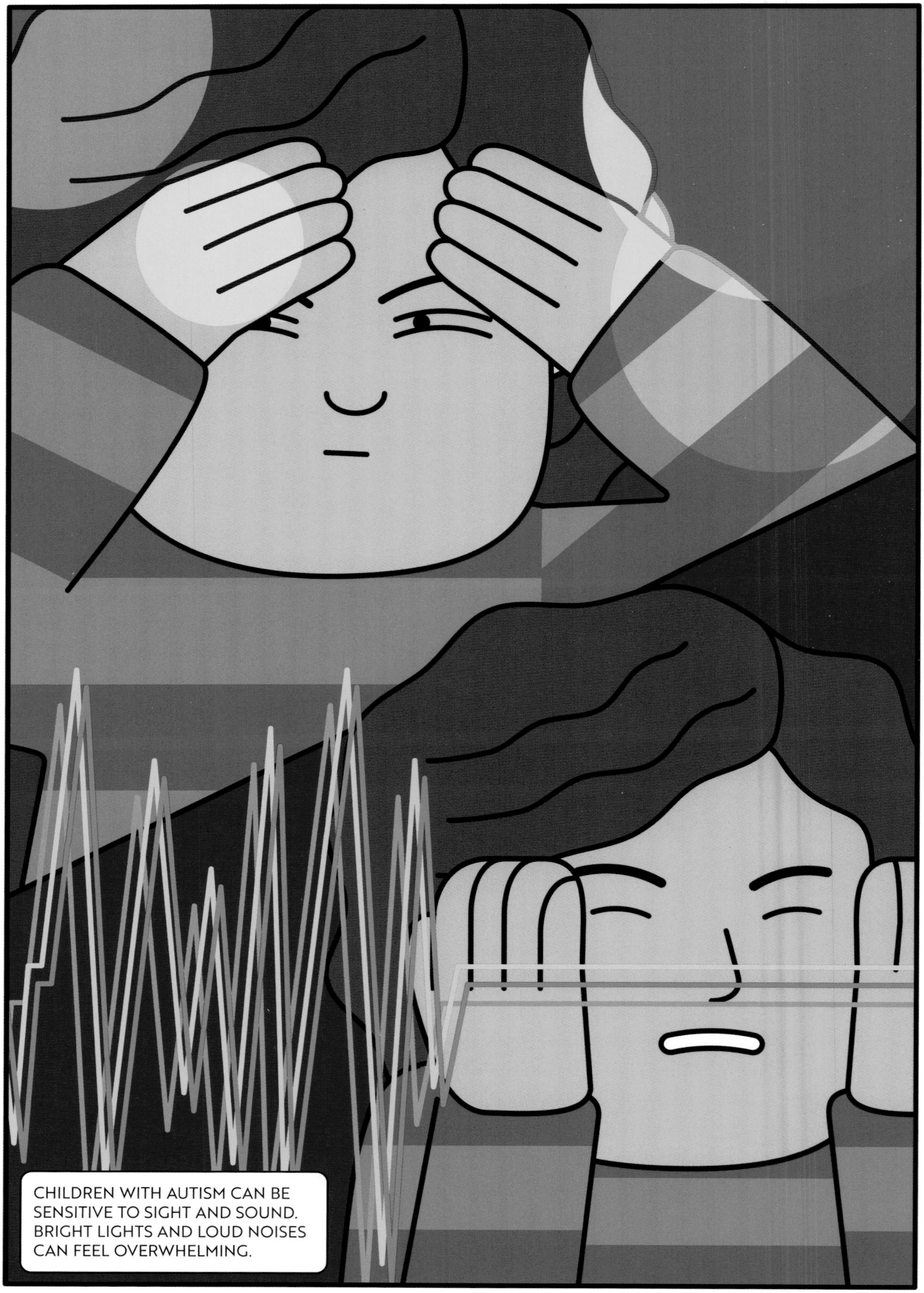
CHILDREN WITH AUTISM CAN BE SENSITIVE TO SIGHT AND SOUND. BRIGHT LIGHTS AND LOUD NOISES CAN FEEL OVERWHELMING.

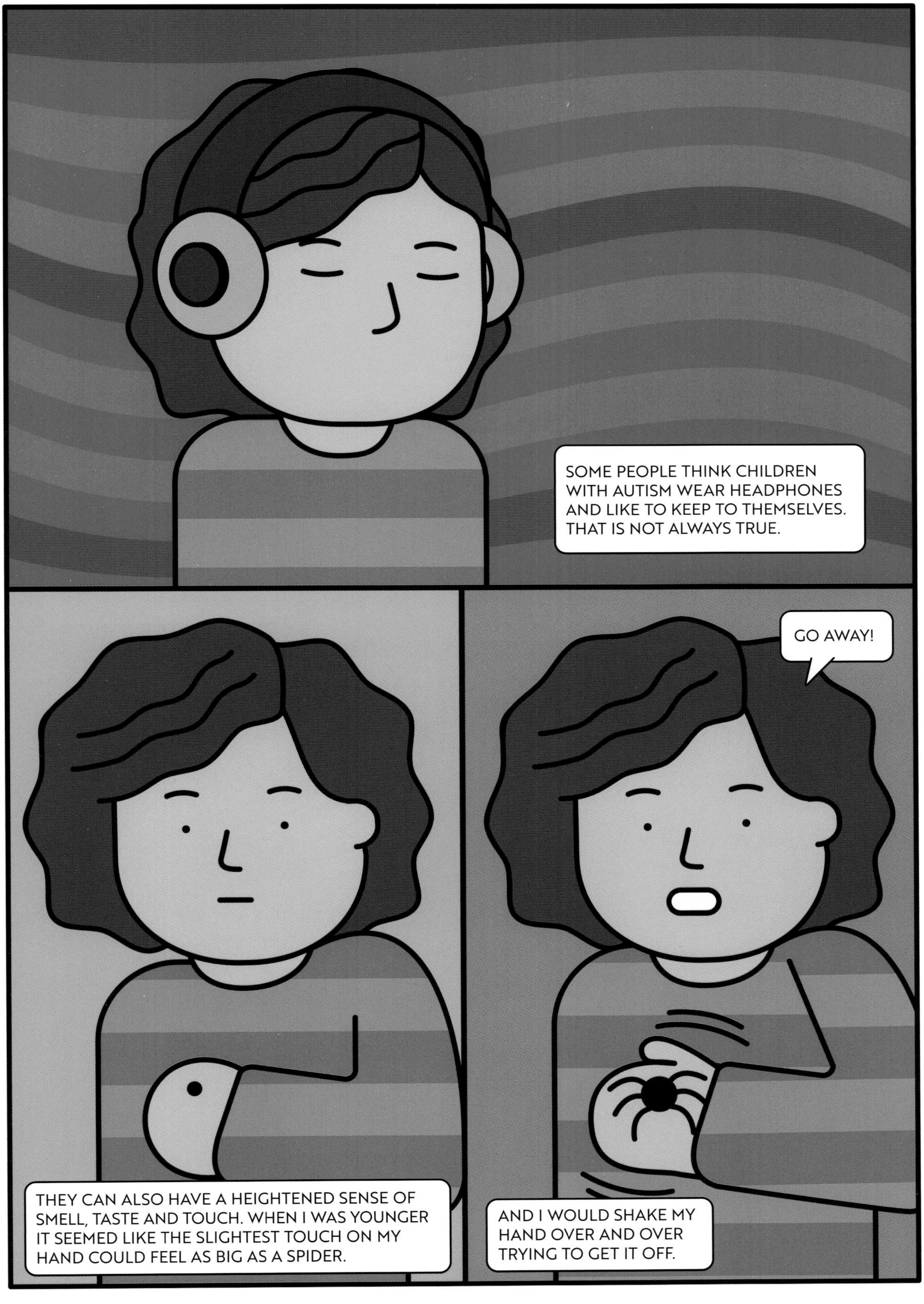
SOME PEOPLE THINK CHILDREN WITH AUTISM WEAR HEADPHONES AND LIKE TO KEEP TO THEMSELVES. THAT IS NOT ALWAYS TRUE.
THEY CAN ALSO HAVE A HEIGHTENED SENSE OF SMELL, TASTE AND TOUCH. WHEN I WAS YOUNGER IT SEEMED LIKE THE SLIGHTEST TOUCH ON MY HAND COULD FEEL AS BIG AS A SPIDER.
GO AWAY!
AND I WOULD SHAKE MY HAND OVER AND OVER TRYING TO GET IT OFF.

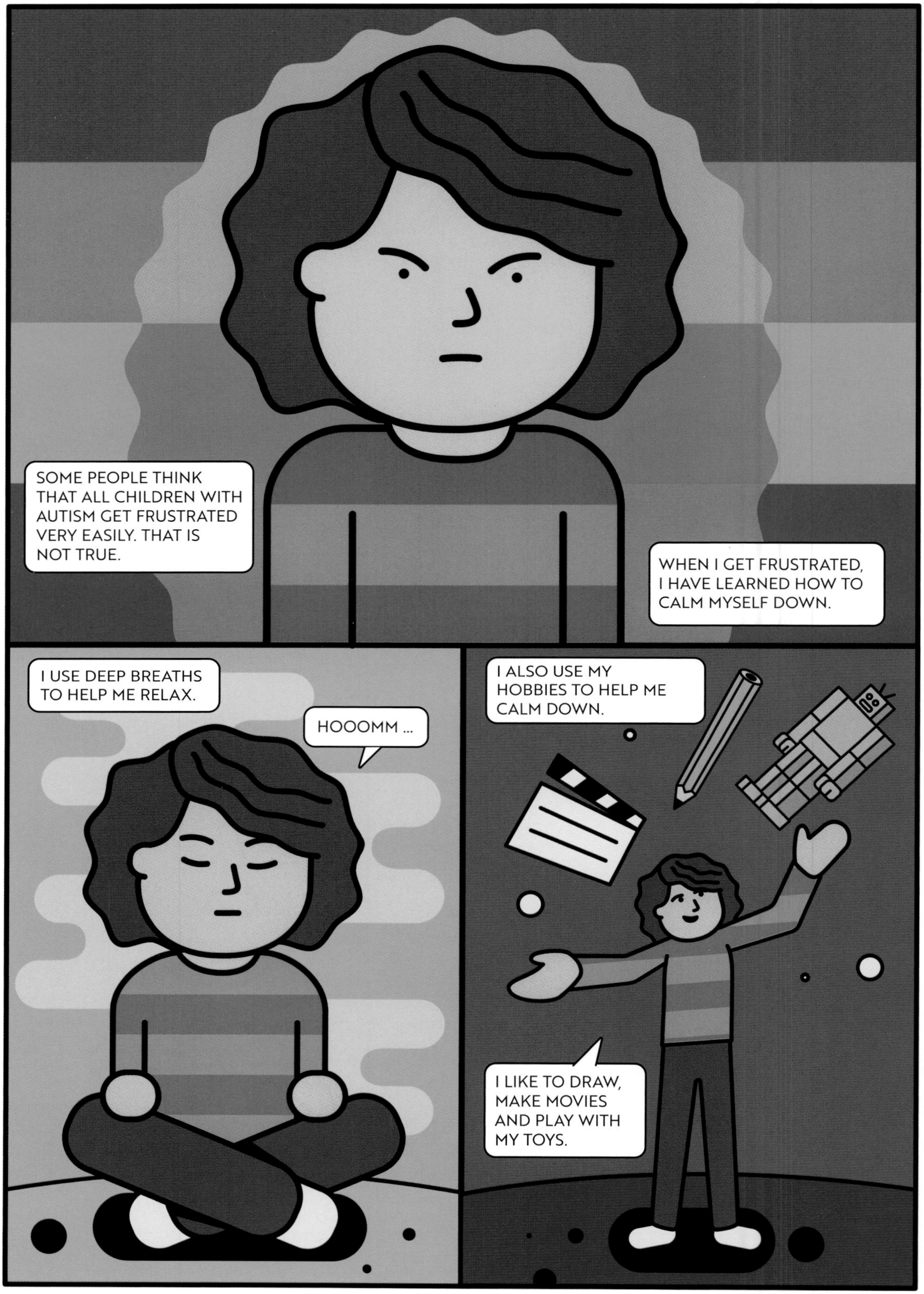
SOME PEOPLE THINK THAT ALL CHILDREN WITH AUTISM GET FRUSTRATED VERY EASILY. THAT IS NOT TRUE.
WHEN I GET FRUSTRATED, I HAVE LEARNED HOW TO CALM MYSELF DOWN.
I USE DEEP BREATHS TO HELP ME RELAX.
HOOOMM ...
I ALSO USE MY HOBBIES TO HELP ME CALM DOWN.
I LIKE TO DRAW, MAKE MOVIES AND PLAY WITH MY TOYS.

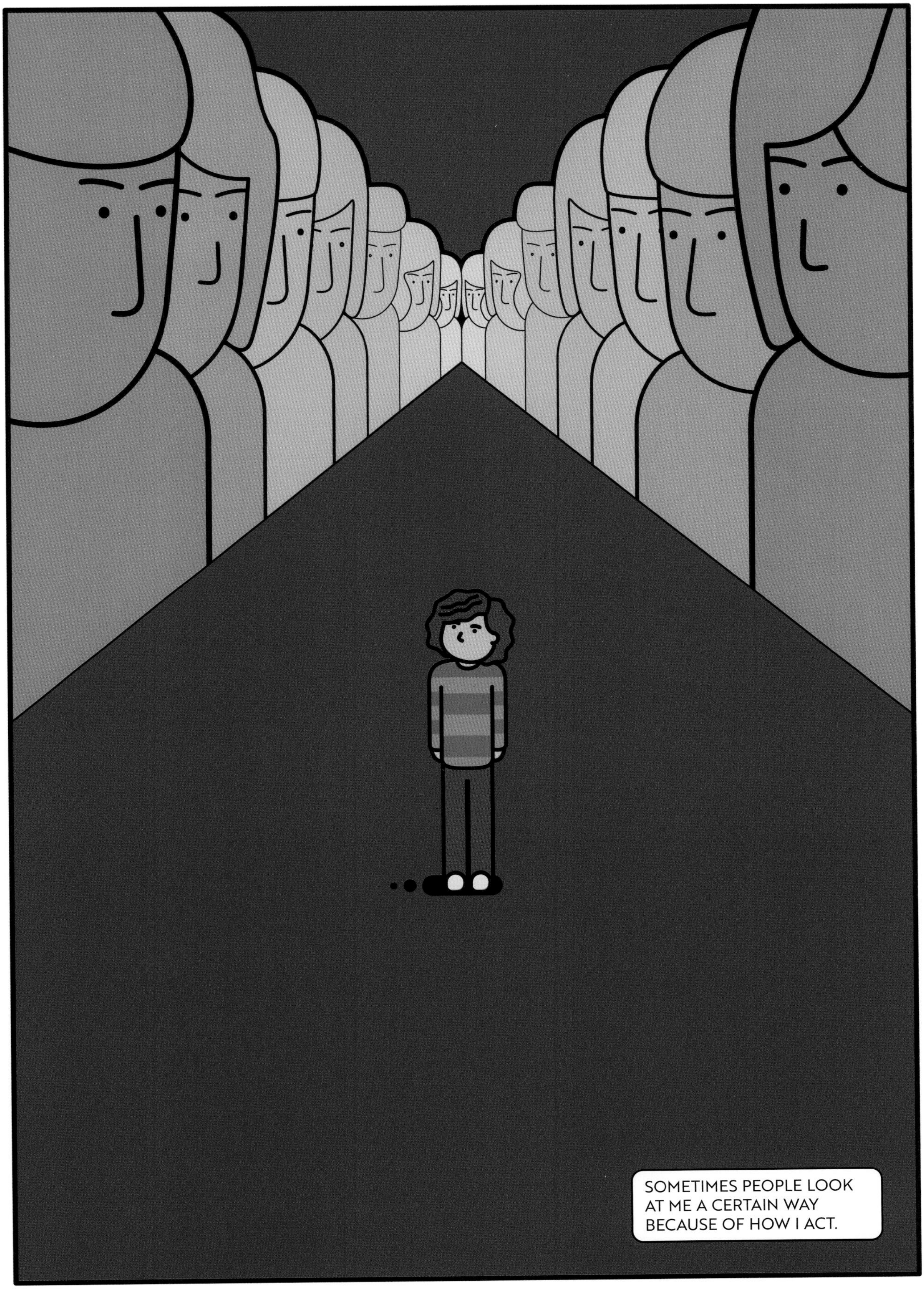
SOMETIMES PEOPLE LOOK
AT ME A CERTAIN WAY
BECAUSE OF HOW I ACT.

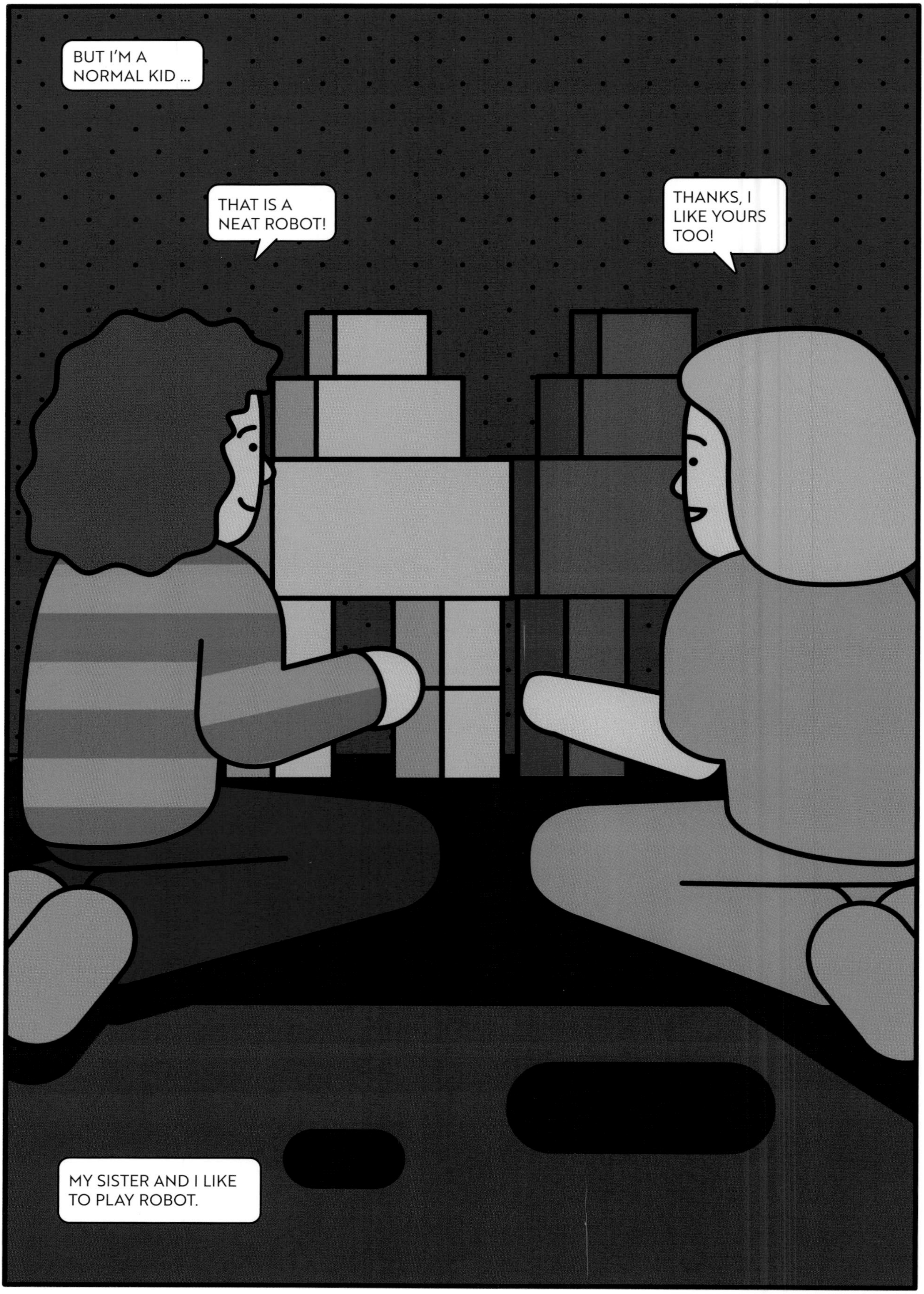
BUT I'M A NORMAL KID ...
THAT IS A NEAT ROBOT!
THANKS, I LIKE YOURS TOO!
MY SISTER AND I LIKE TO PLAY ROBOT.

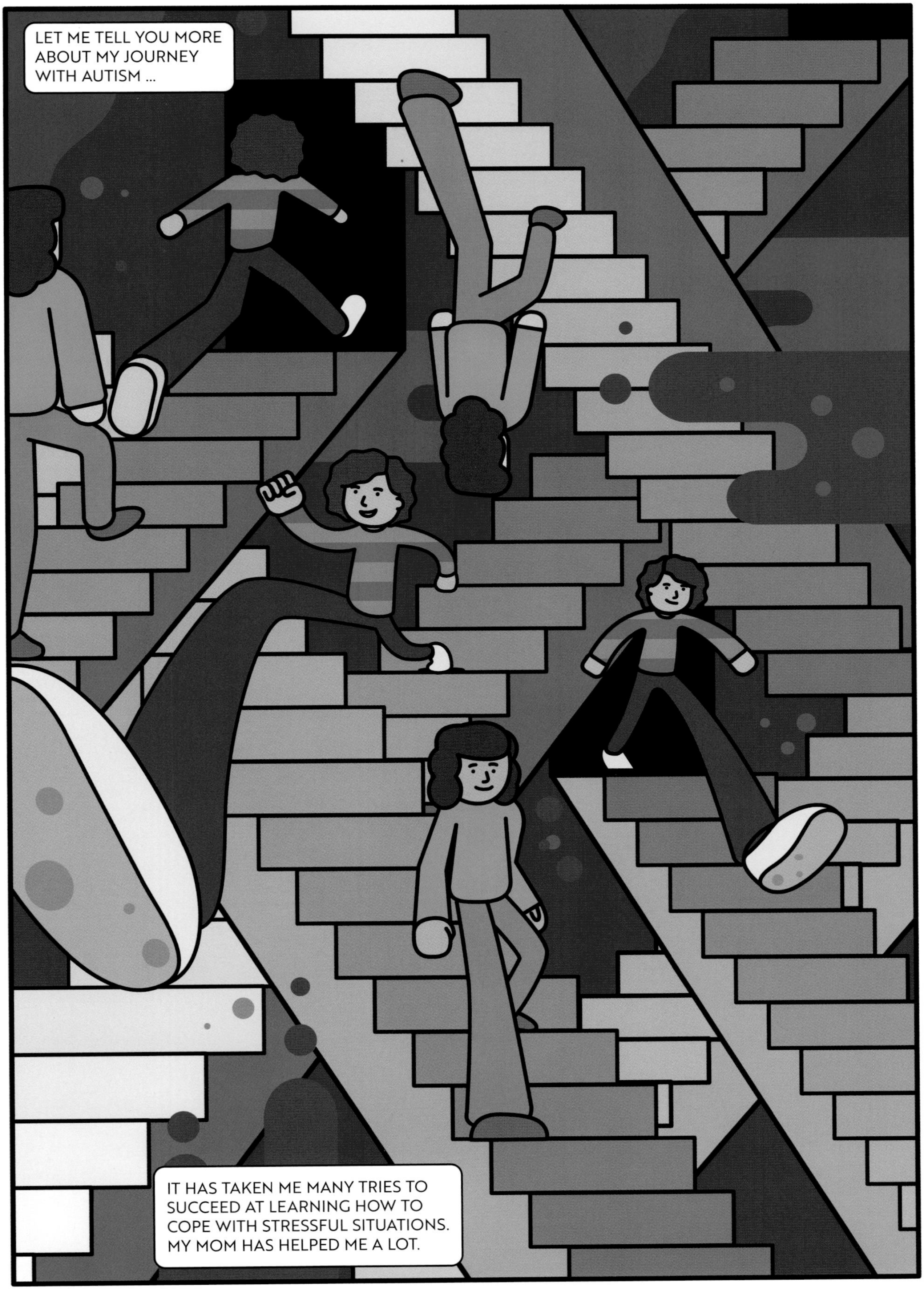
LET ME TELL YOU MORE ABOUT MY JOURNEY WITH AUTISM ...
IT HAS TAKEN ME MANY TRIES TO SUCCEED AT LEARNING HOW TO COPE WITH STRESSFUL SITUATIONS. MY MOM HAS HELPED ME A LOT.

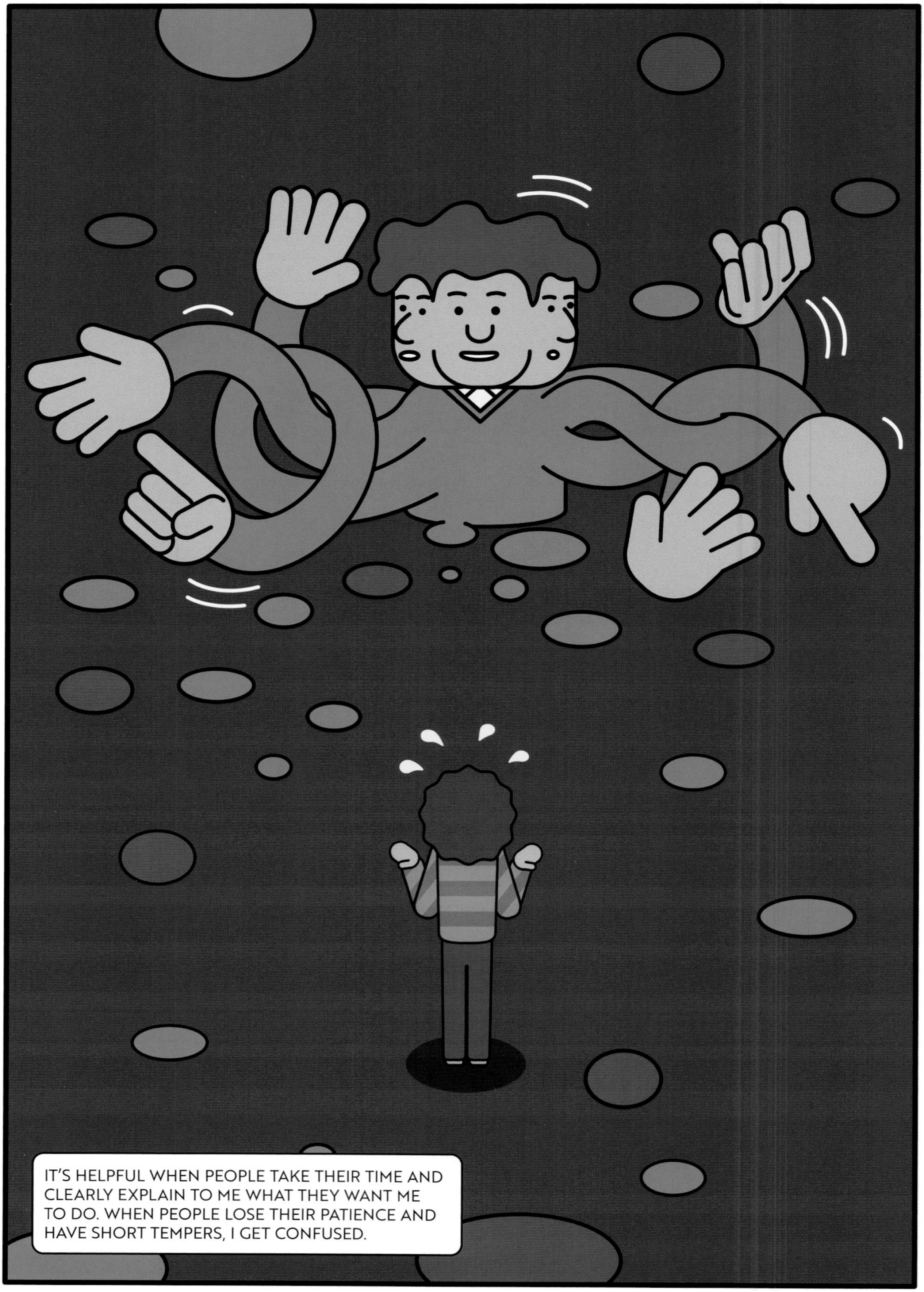
IT'S HELPFUL WHEN PEOPLE TAKE THEIR TIME AND CLEARLY EXPLAIN TO ME WHAT THEY WANT ME TO DO. WHEN PEOPLE LOSE THEIR PATIENCE AND HAVE SHORT TEMPERS, I GET CONFUSED.

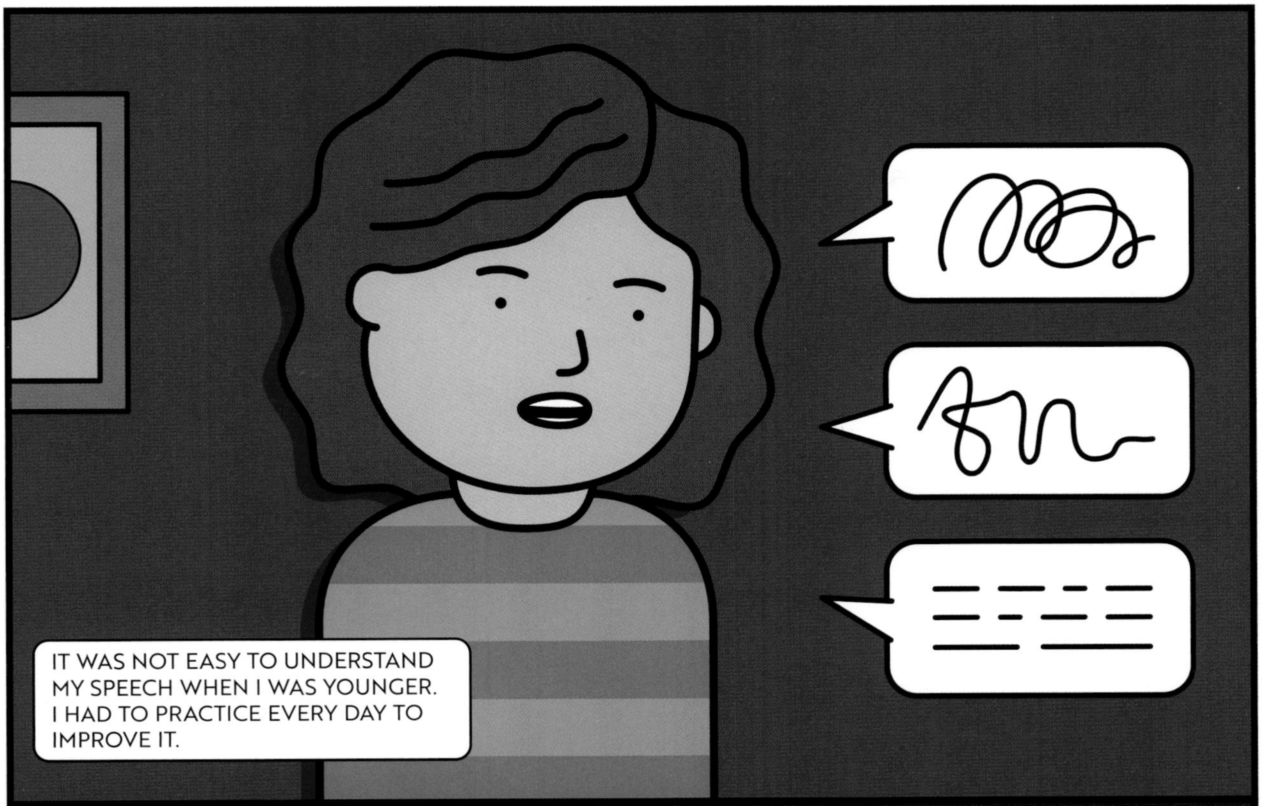
IT WAS NOT EASY TO UNDERSTAND MY SPEECH WHEN I WAS YOUNGER. I HAD TO PRACTICE EVERY DAY TO IMPROVE IT.

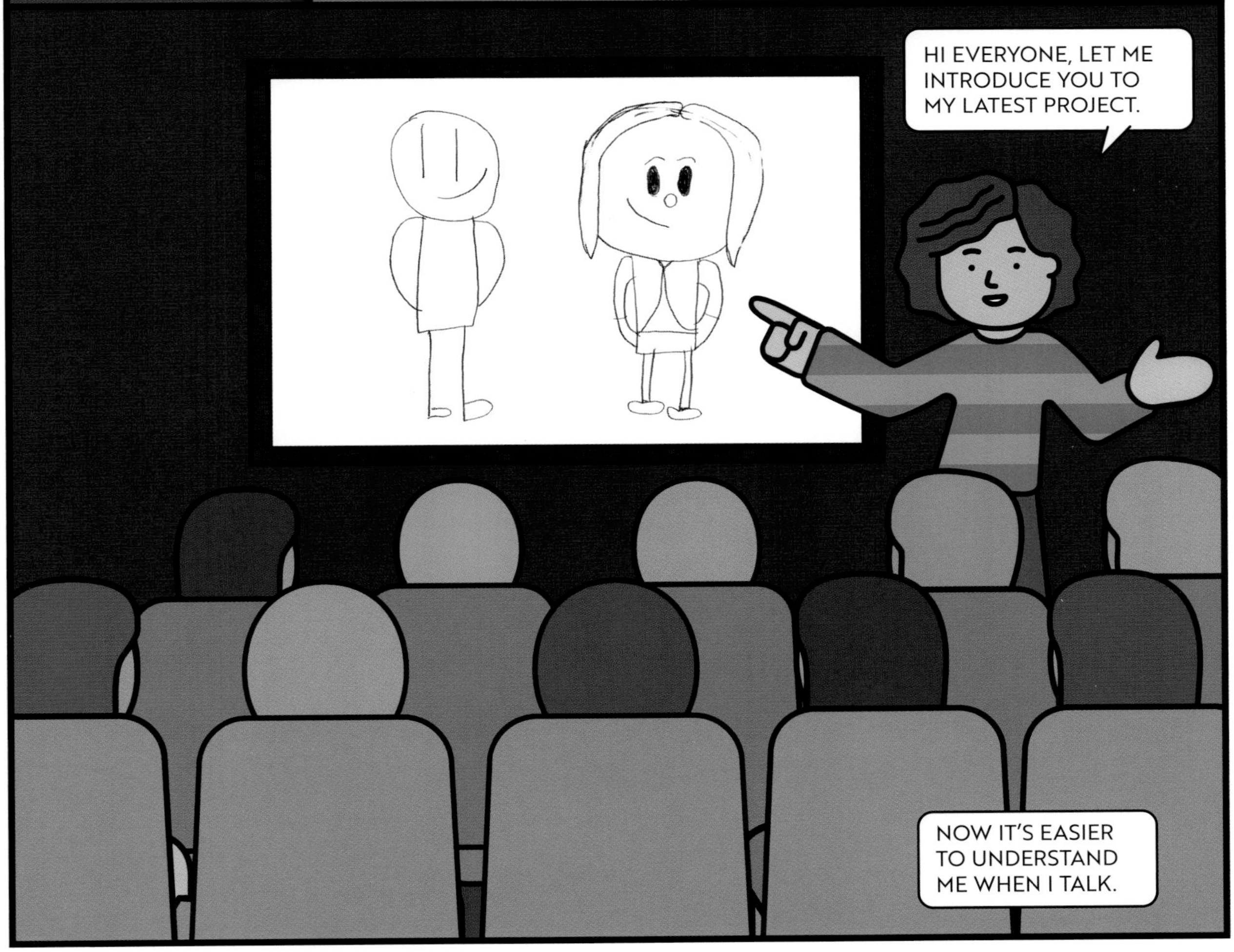
HI EVERYONE, LET ME INTRODUCE YOU TO MY LATEST PROJECT.
NOW IT'S EASIER TO UNDERSTAND ME WHEN I TALK.

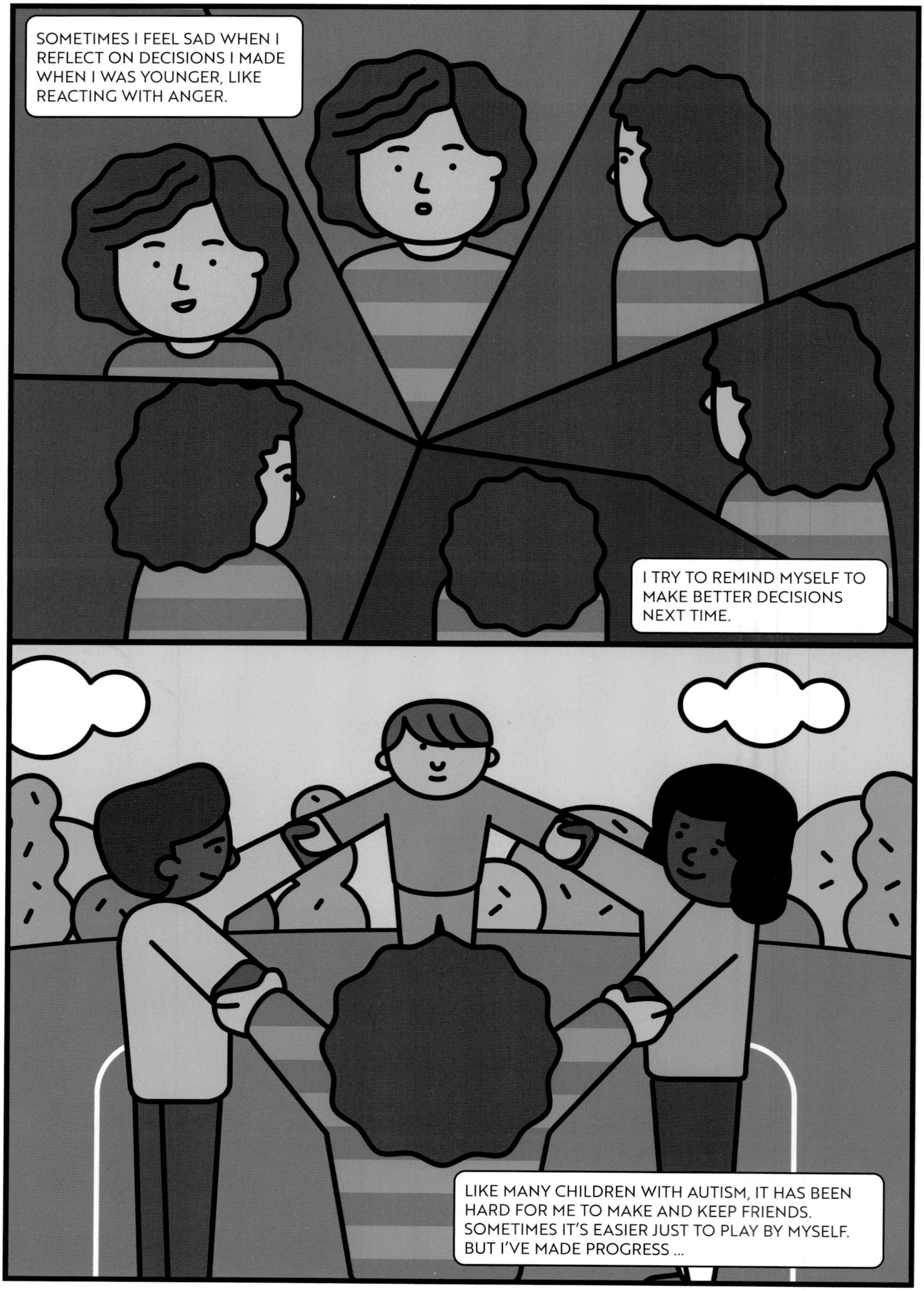
SOMETIMES I FEEL SAD WHEN I REFLECT ON DECISIONS I MADE WHEN I WAS YOUNGER, LIKE REACTING WITH ANGER.
I TRY TO REMIND MYSELF TO MAKE BETTER DECISIONS NEXT TIME.
LIKE MANY CHILDREN WITH AUTISM, IT HAS BEEN HARD FOR ME TO MAKE AND KEEP FRIENDS. SOMETIMES IT'S EASIER JUST TO PLAY BY MYSELF. BUT I'VE MADE PROGRESS ...

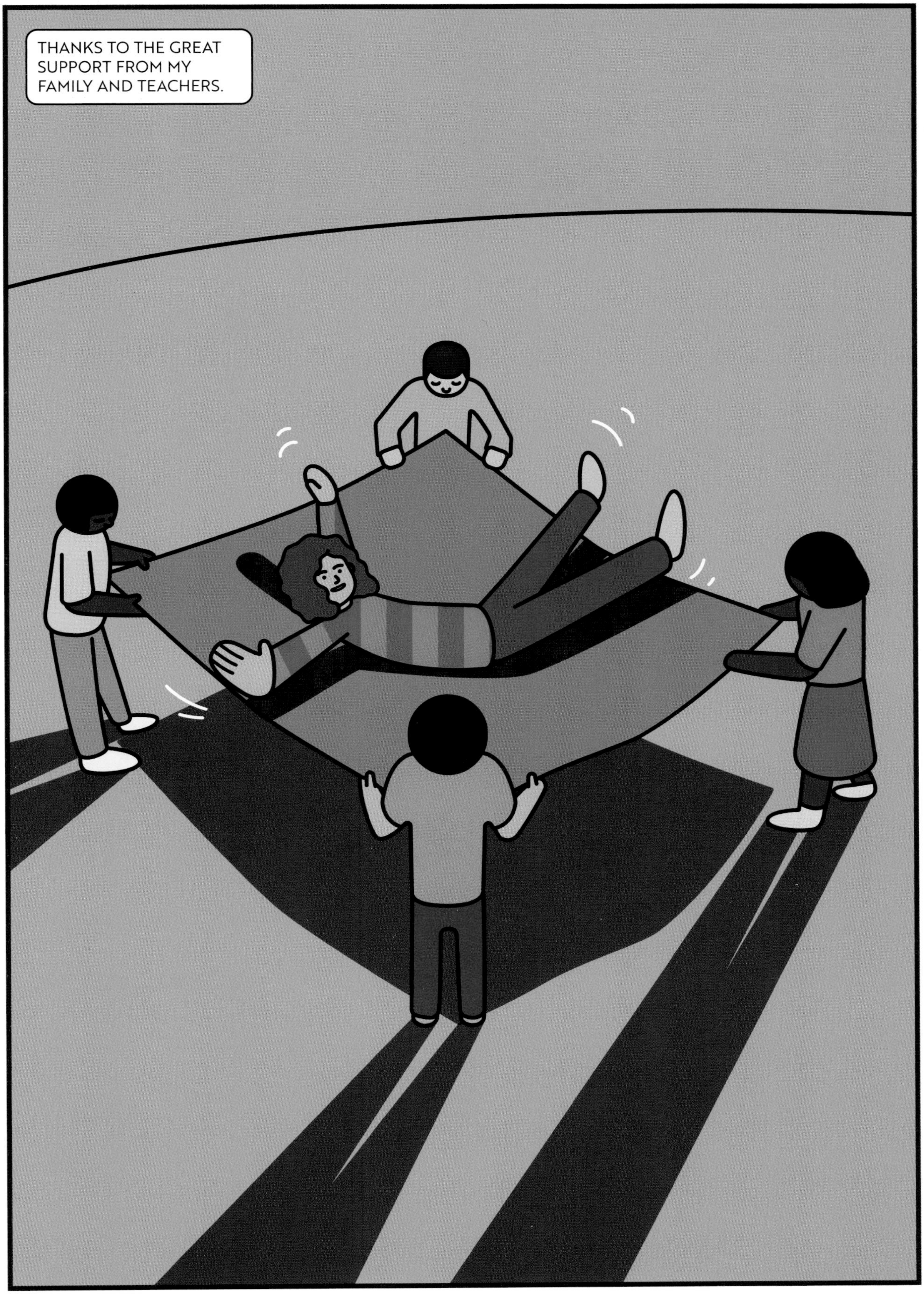
THANKS TO THE GREAT SUPPORT FROM MY FAMILY AND TEACHERS.

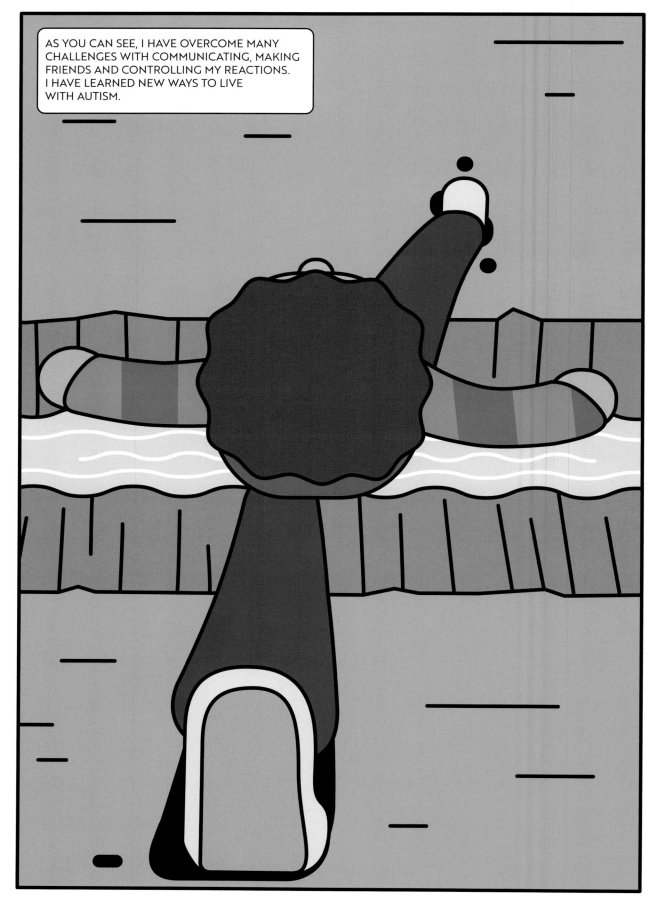

AS YOU CAN SEE, I HAVE OVERCOME MANY CHALLENGES WITH COMMUNICATING, MAKING FRIENDS AND CONTROLLING MY REACTIONS. I HAVE LEARNED NEW WAYS TO LIVE WITH AUTISM.

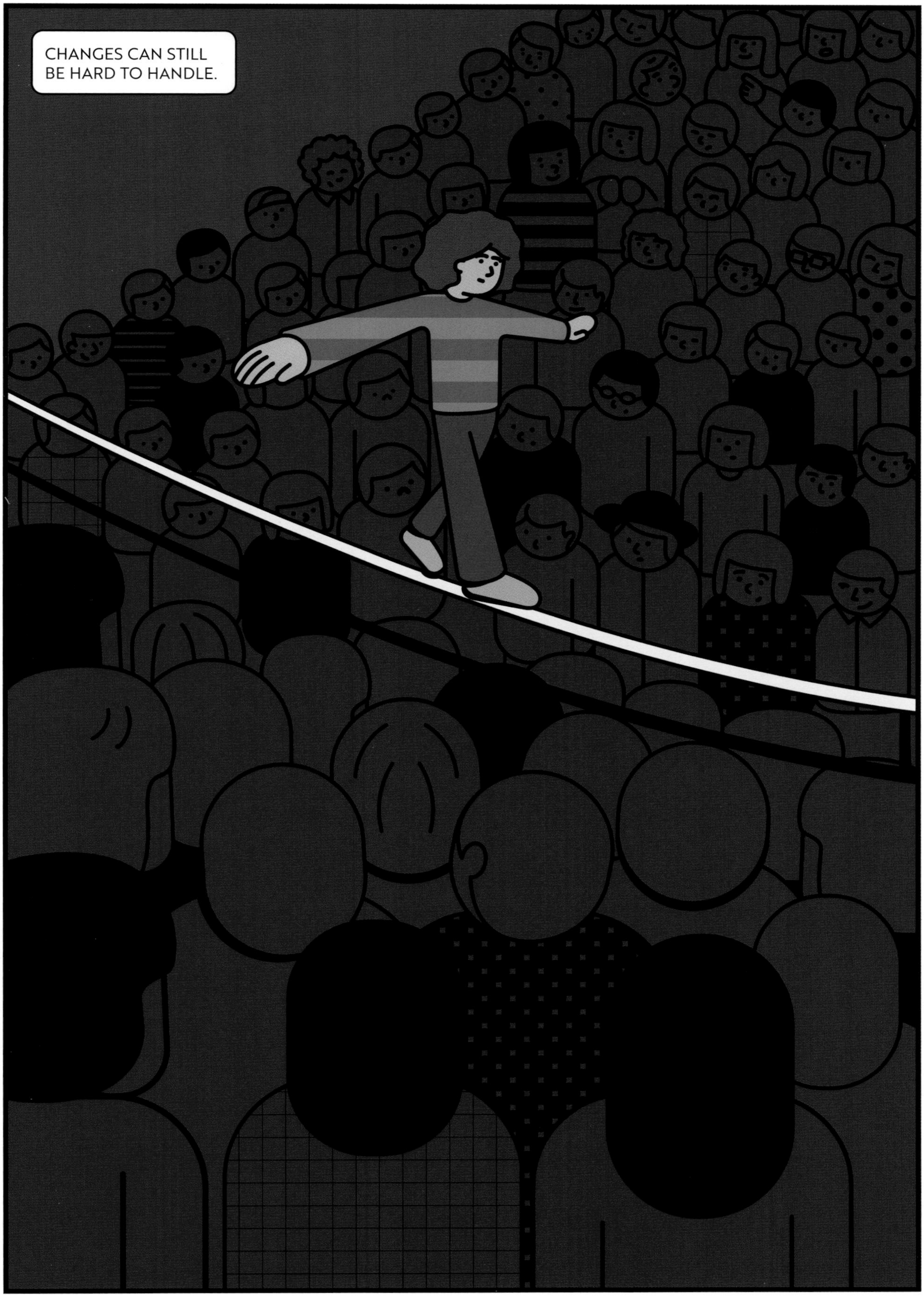
CHANGES CAN STILL BE HARD TO HANDLE.

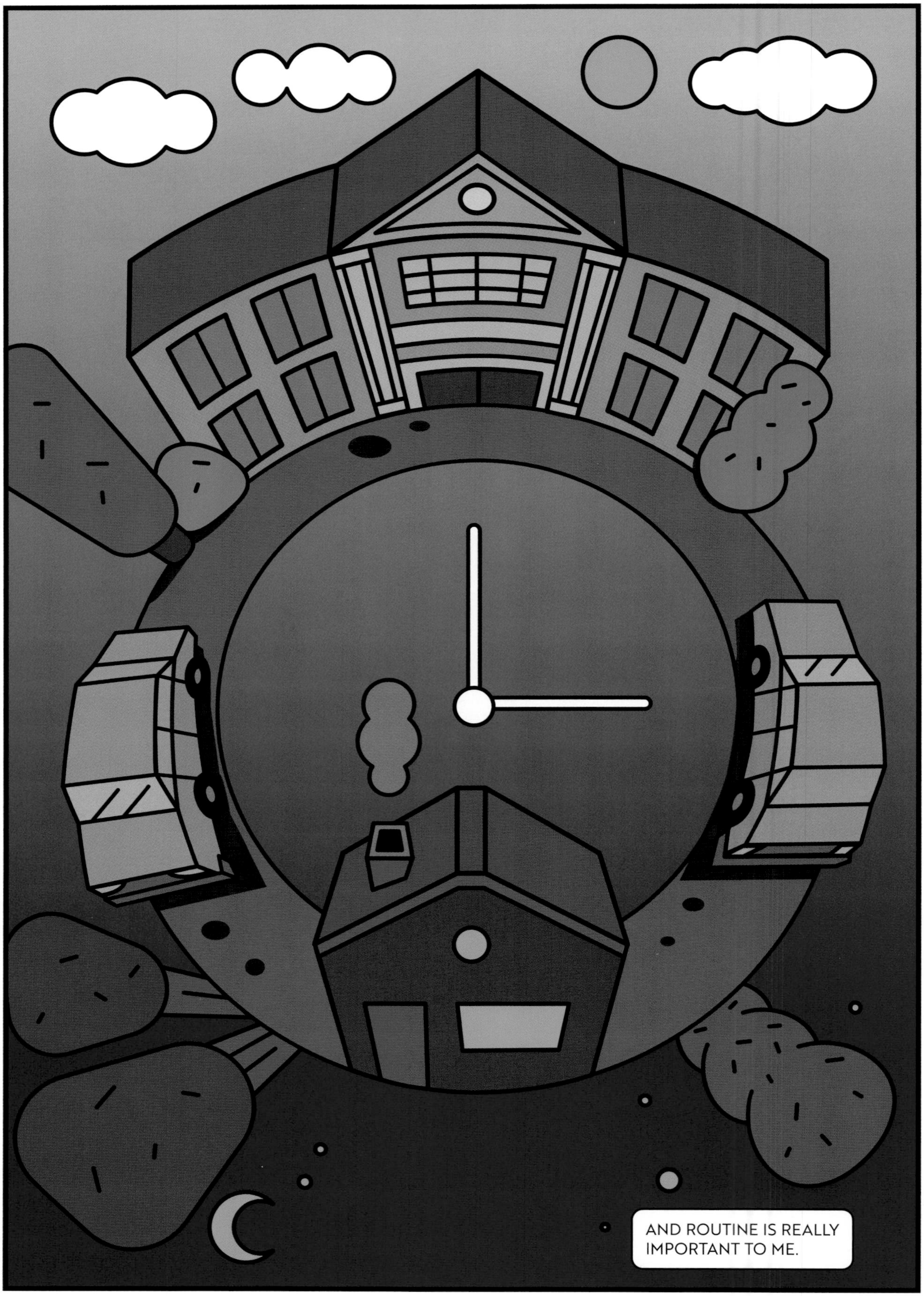
AND ROUTINE IS REALLY IMPORTANT TO ME.

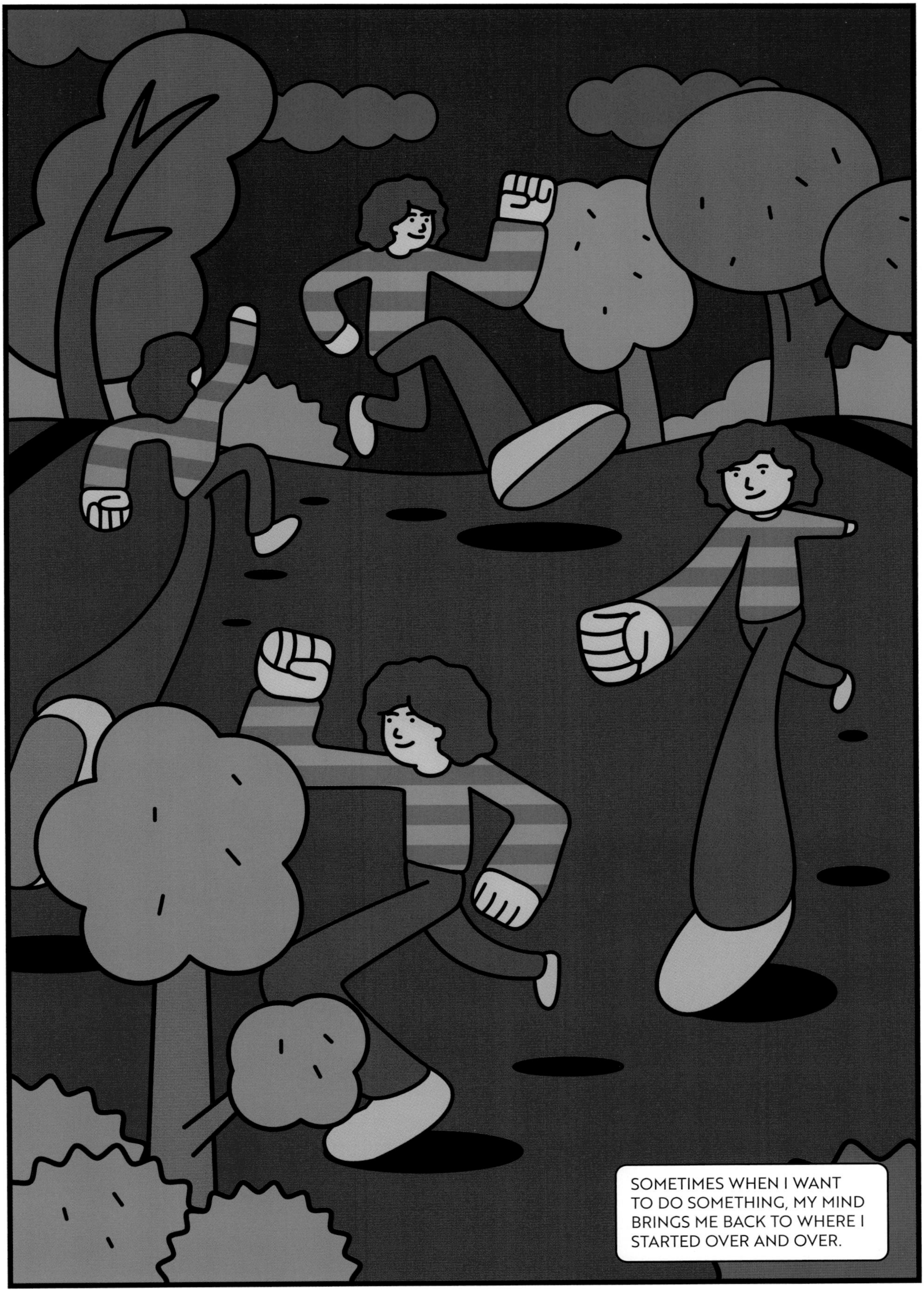
SOMETIMES WHEN I WANT
TO DO SOMETHING, MY MIND
BRINGS ME BACK TO WHERE I
STARTED OVER AND OVER.

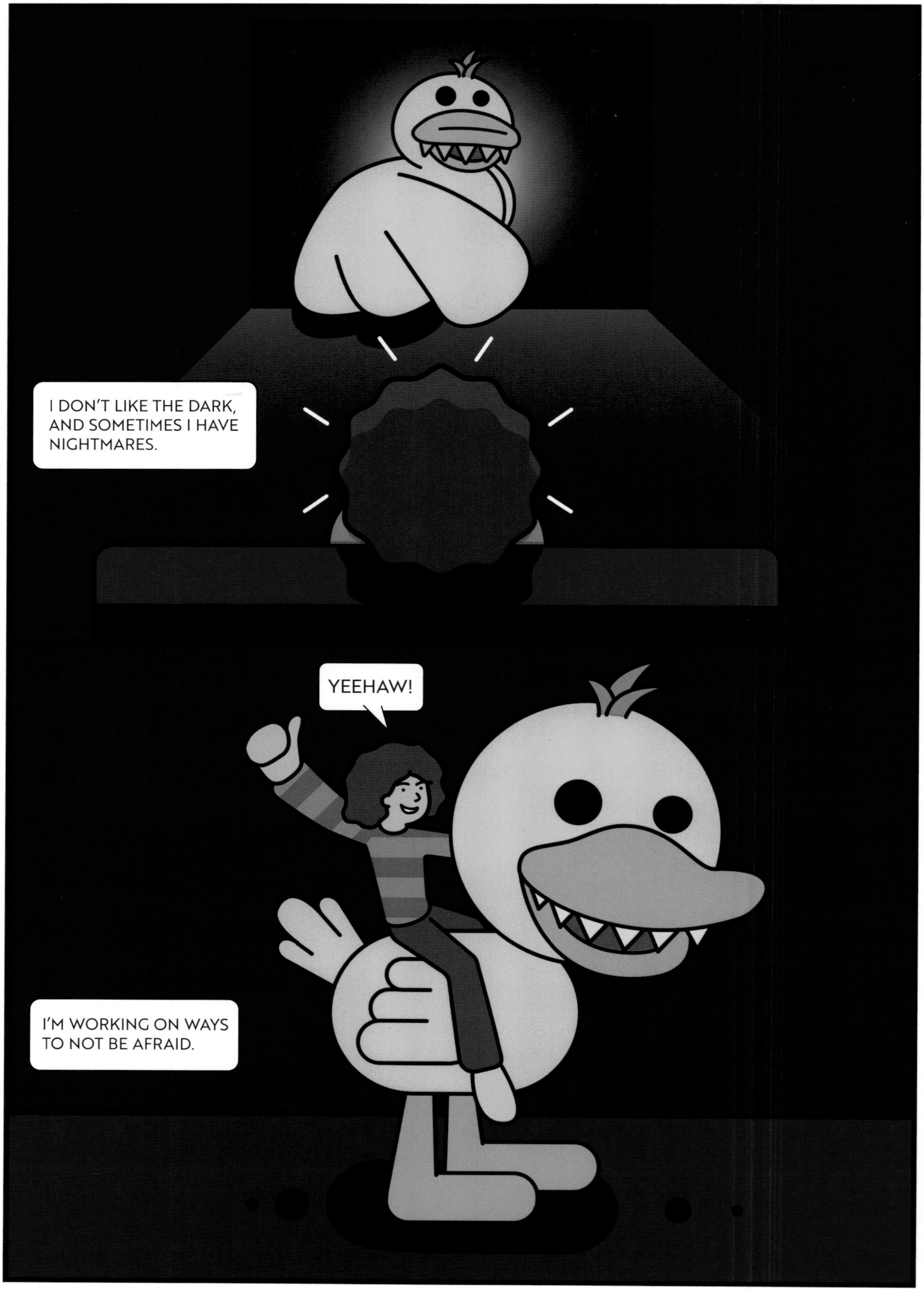
I DON'T LIKE THE DARK, AND SOMETIMES I HAVE NIGHTMARES.
YEEHAW!
I'M WORKING ON WAYS TO NOT BE AFRAID.

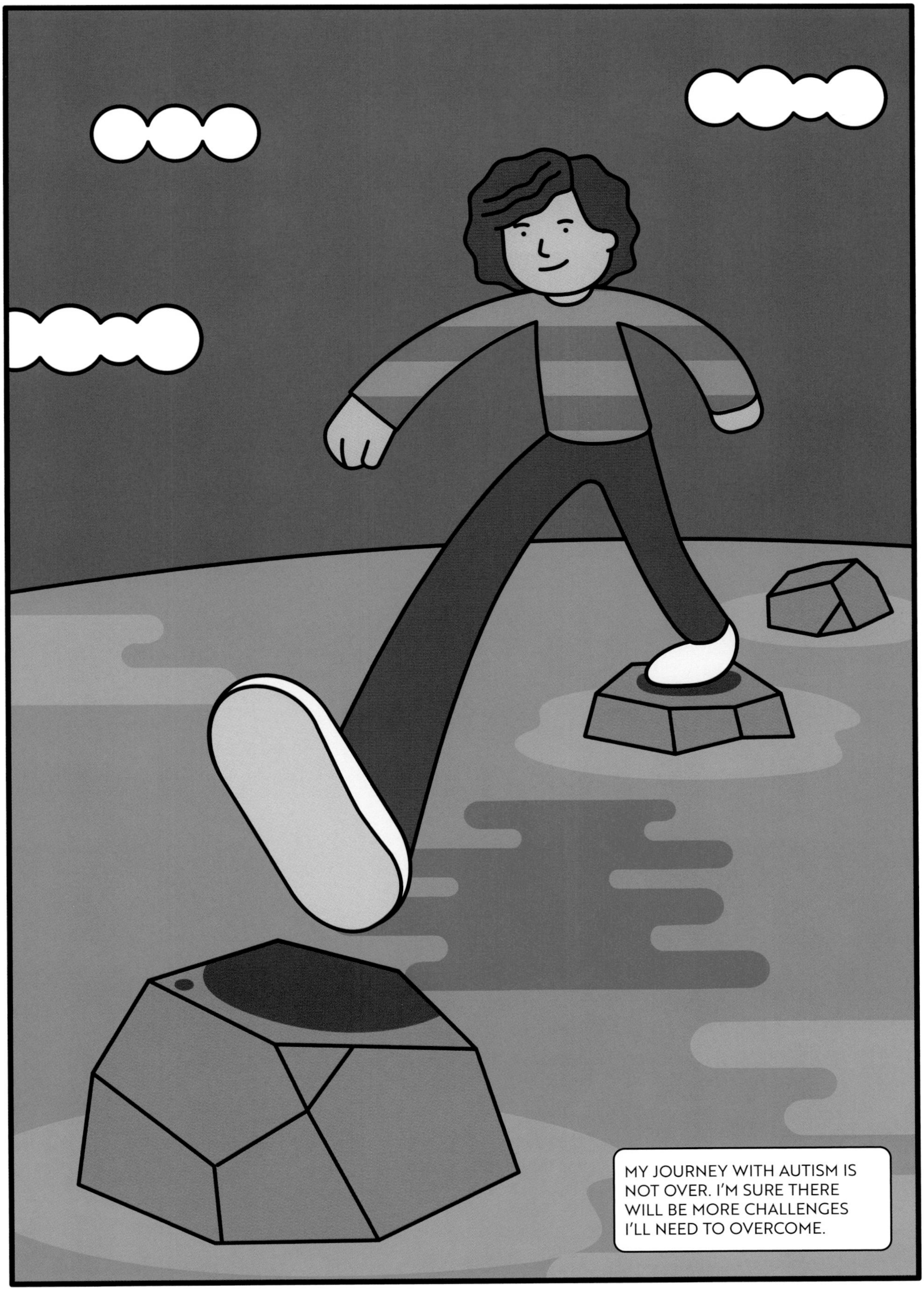
MY JOURNEY WITH AUTISM IS NOT OVER. I'M SURE THERE WILL BE MORE CHALLENGES I'LL NEED TO OVERCOME.

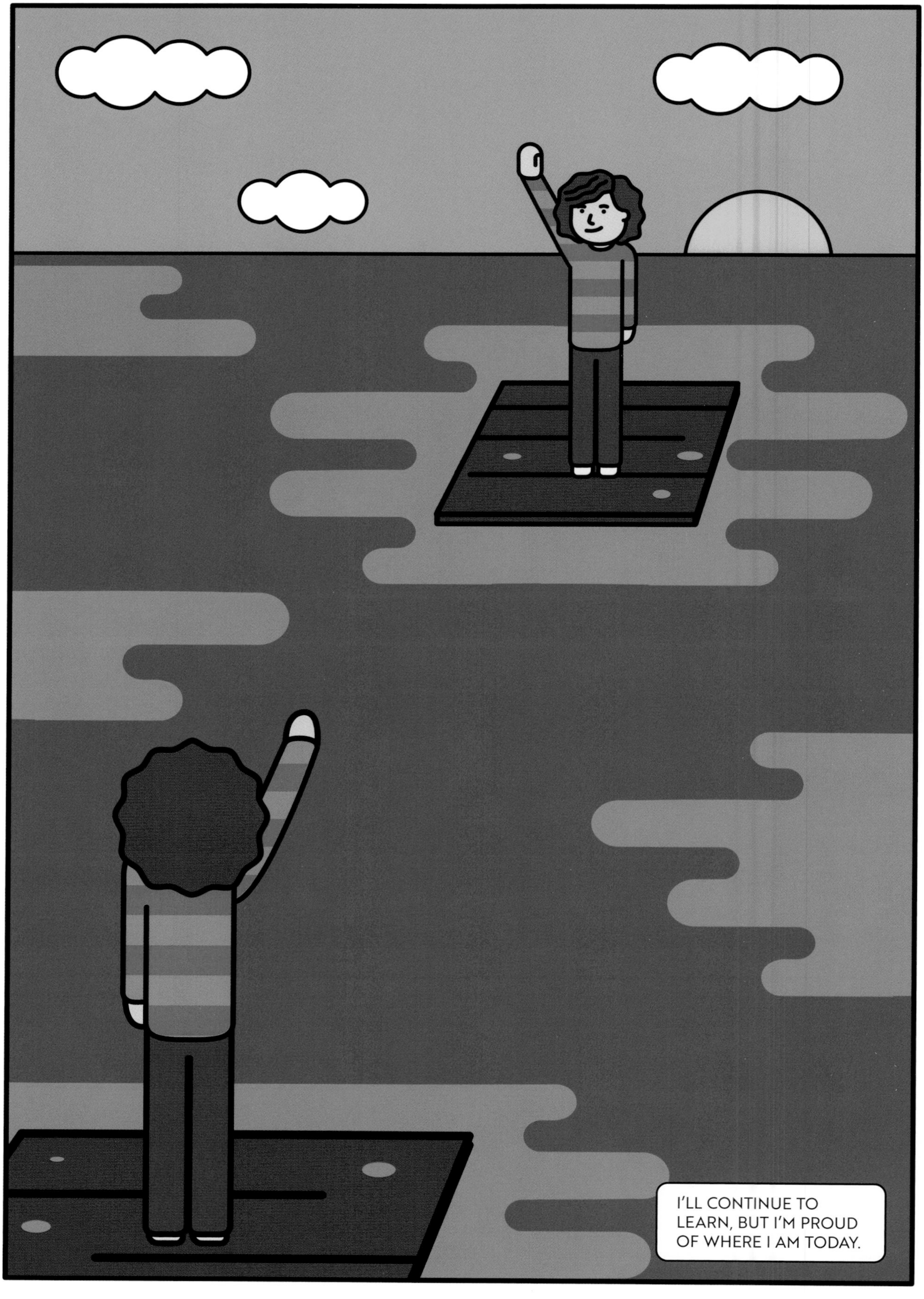
I'LL CONTINUE TO LEARN, BUT I'M PROUD OF WHERE I AM TODAY.

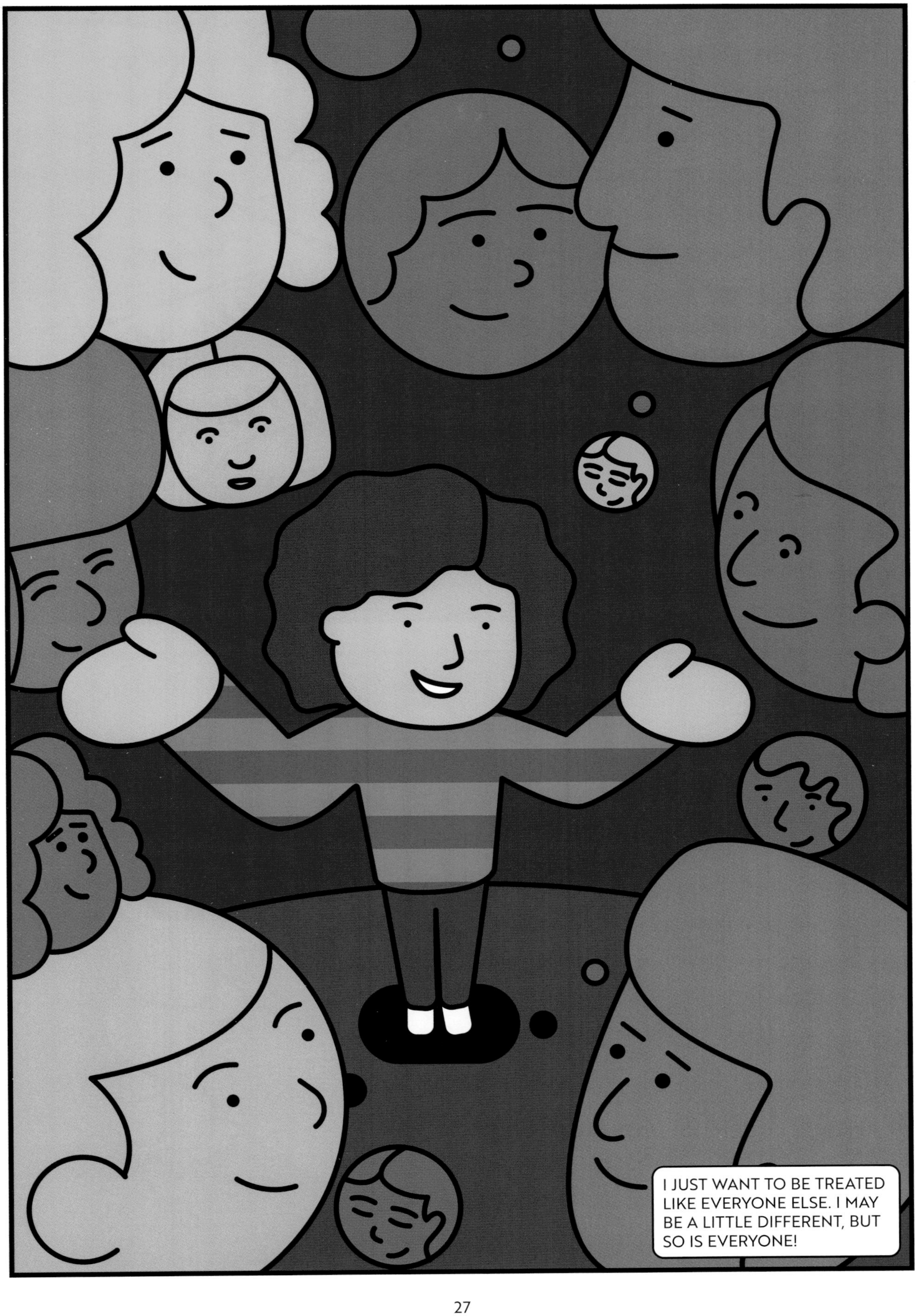
I JUST WANT TO BE TREATED LIKE EVERYONE ELSE. I MAY BE A LITTLE DIFFERENT, BUT SO IS EVERYONE!

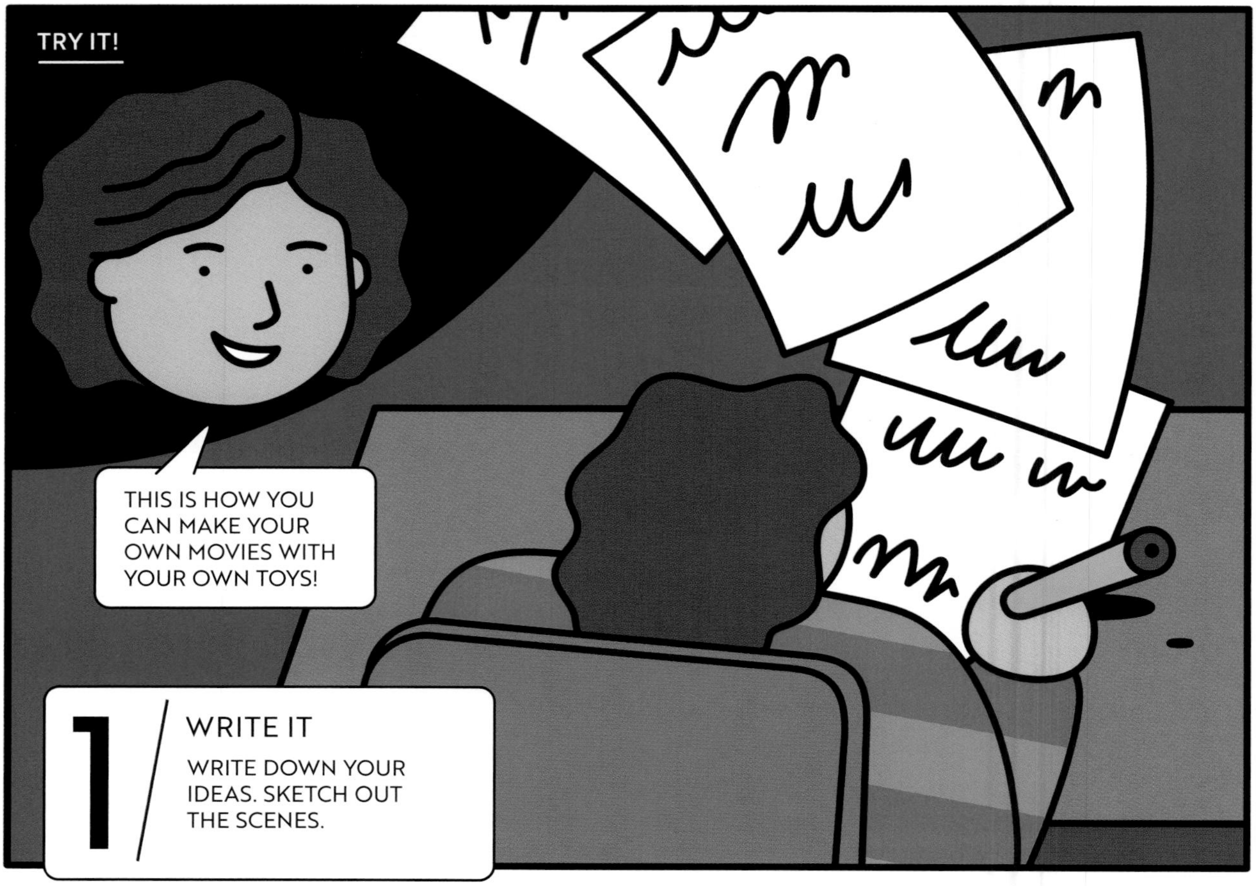
TRY IT!
THIS IS HOW YOU CAN MAKE YOUR OWN MOVIES WITH YOUR OWN TOYS!
1/ WRITE IT
WRITE DOWN YOUR IDEAS. SKETCH OUT THE SCENES.

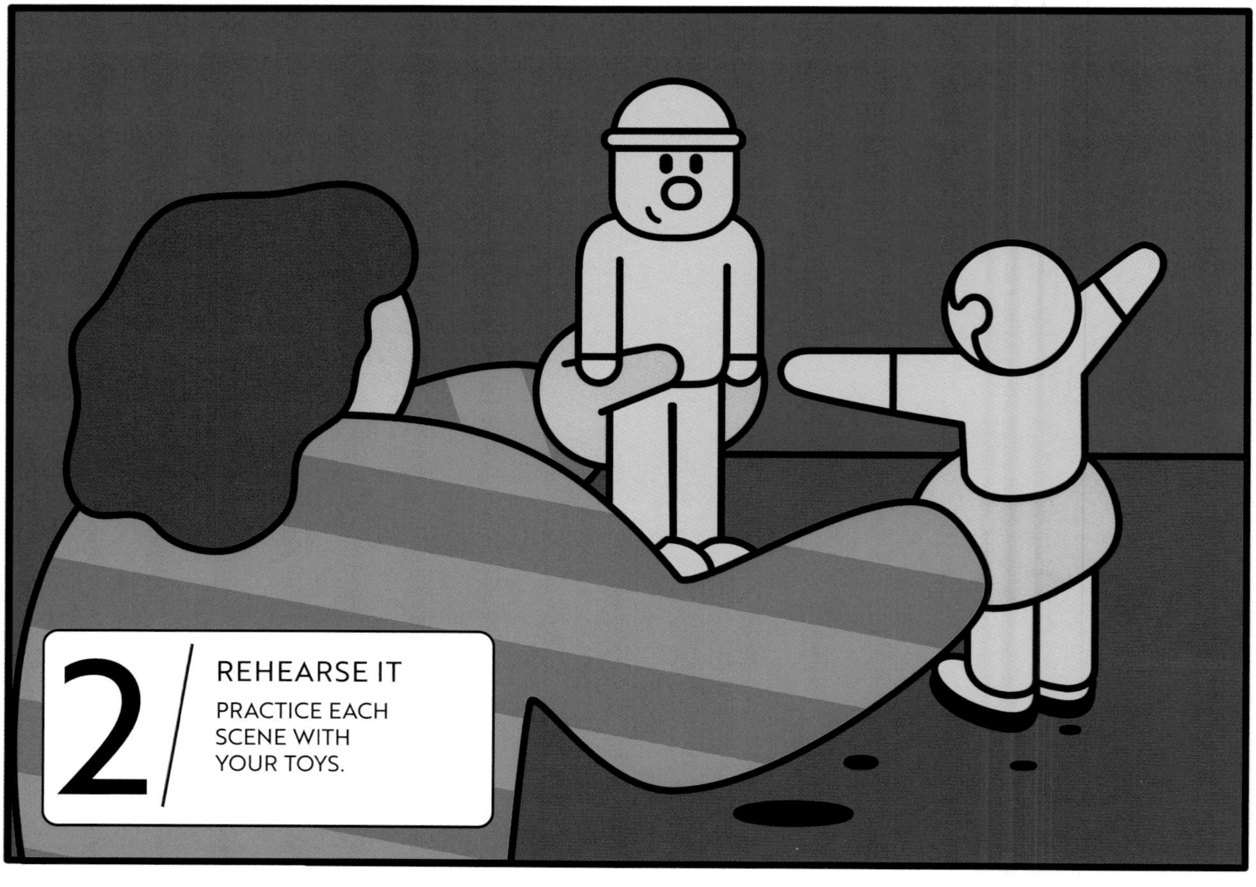
2/ REHEARSE IT
PRACTICE EACH SCENE WITH YOUR TOYS.

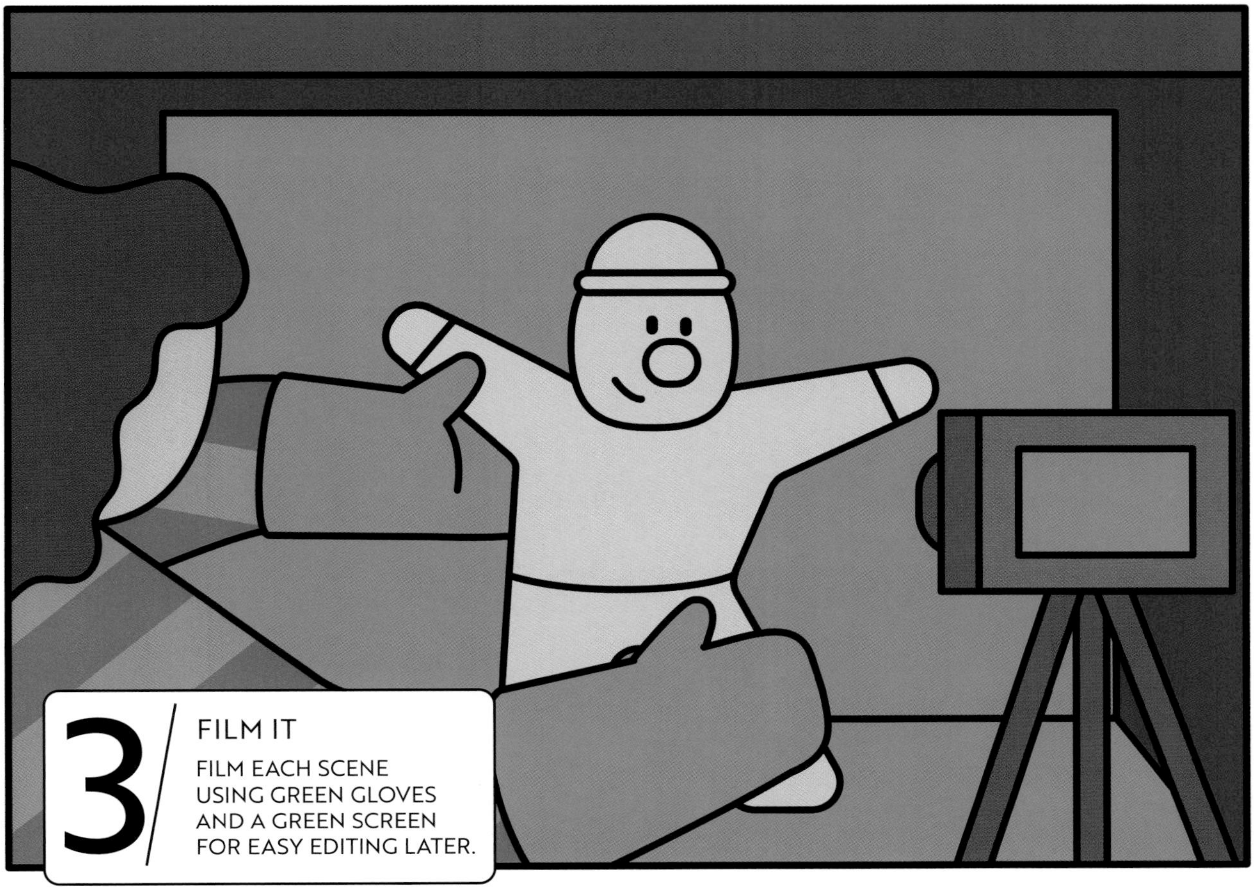
3/
FILM IT
FILM EACH SCENE USING GREEN GLOVES AND A GREEN SCREEN FOR EASY EDITING LATER.

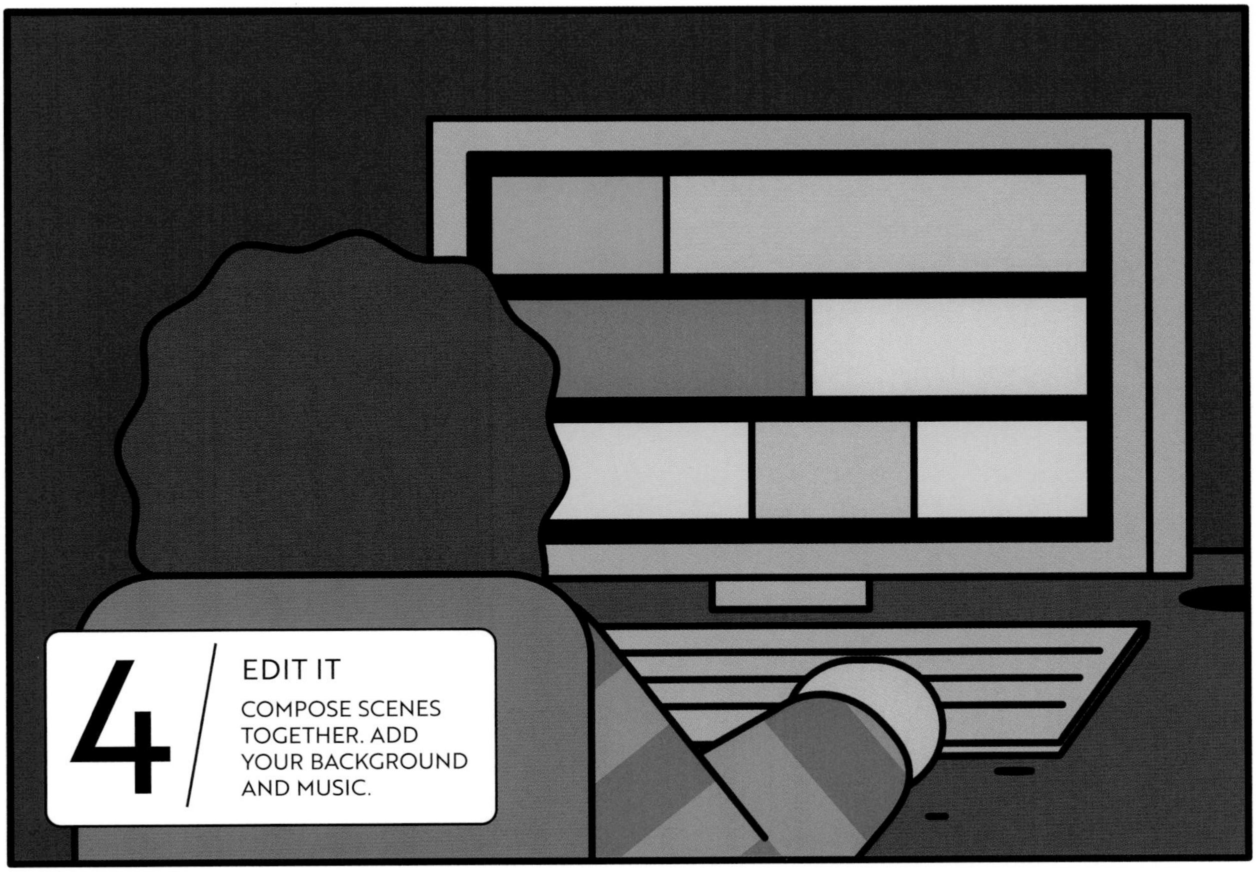
4/
EDIT IT
COMPOSE SCENES TOGETHER. ADD YOUR BACKGROUND AND MUSIC.

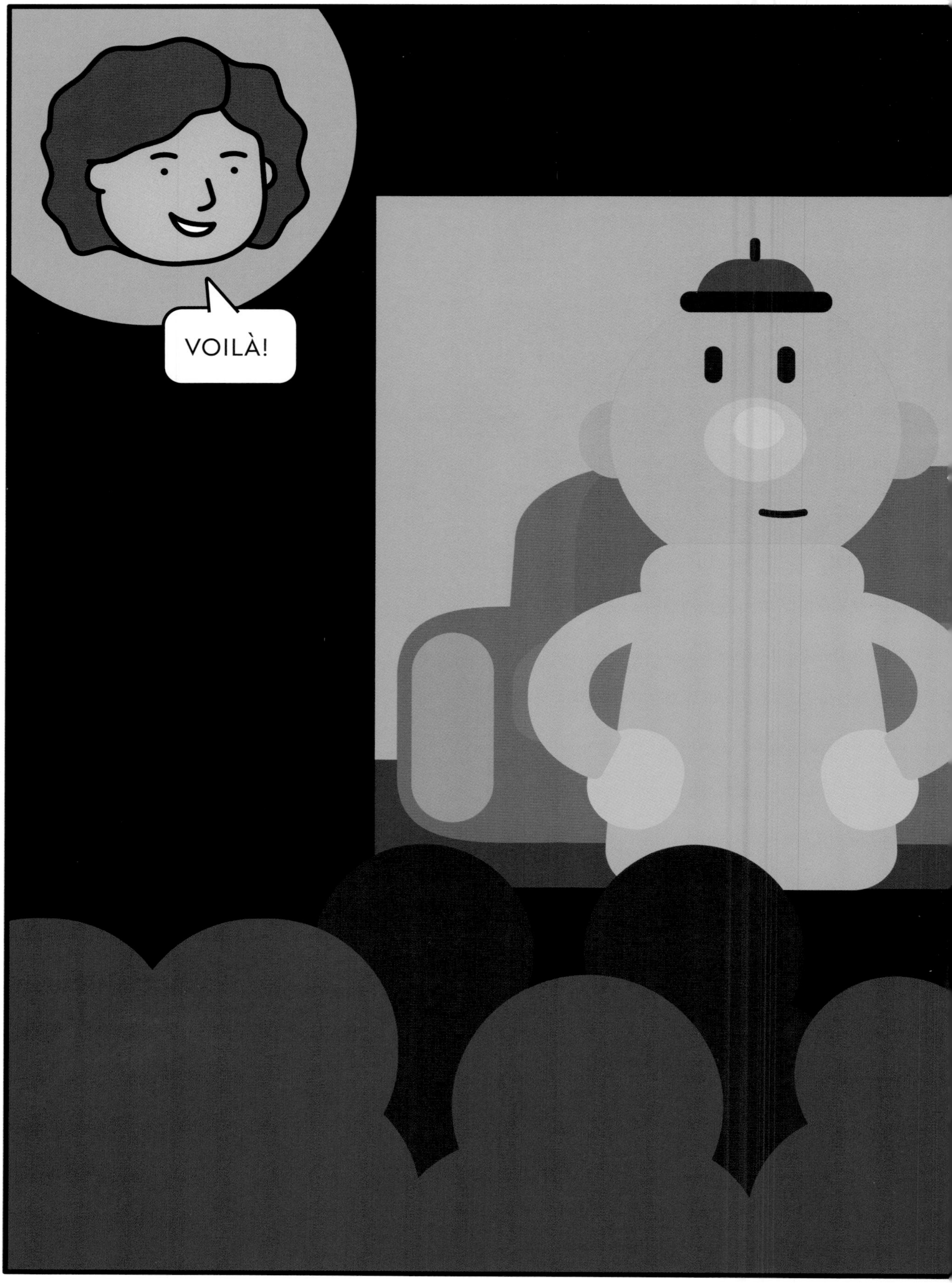
VOILÀ!

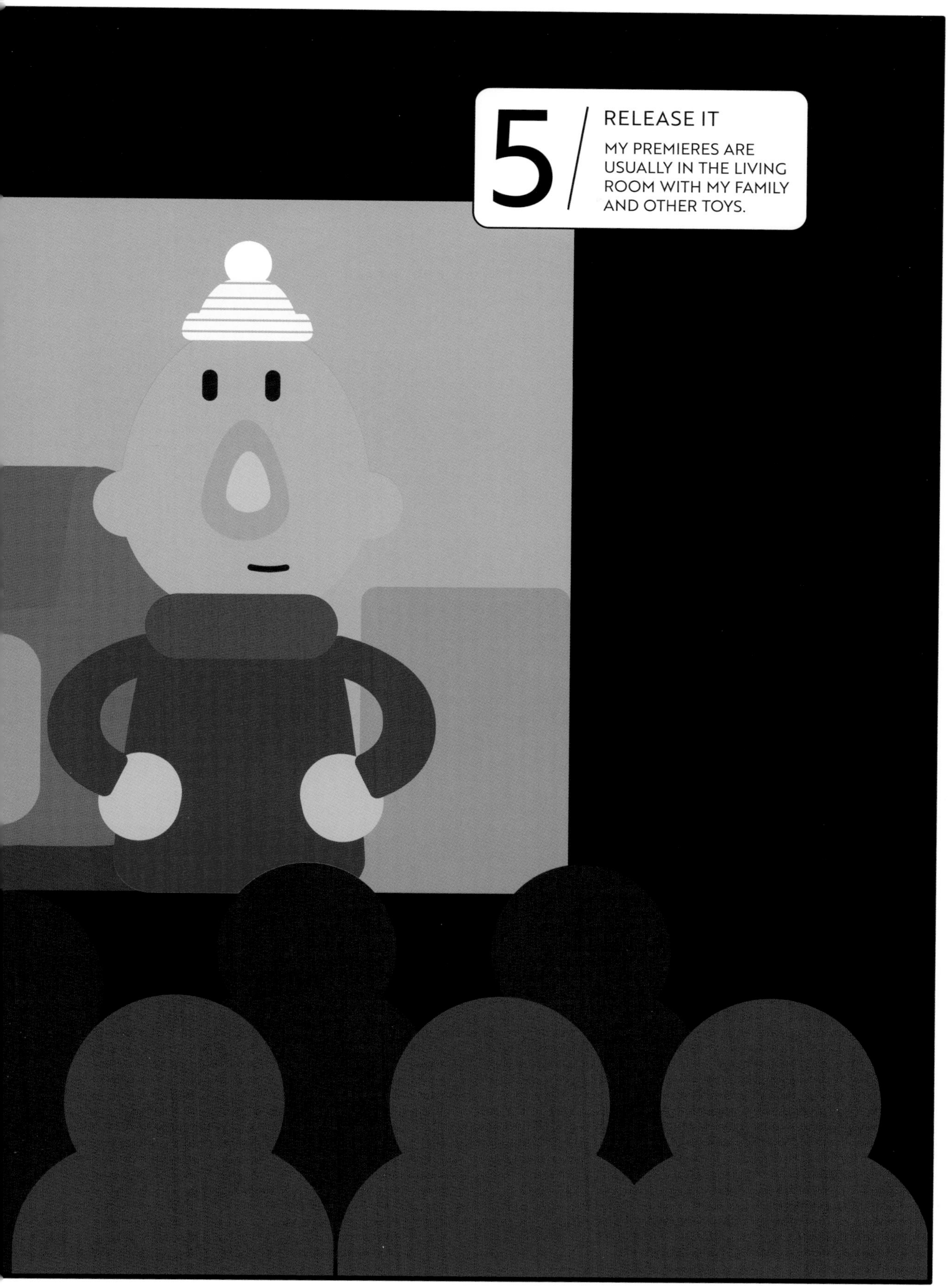

5/ RELEASE IT

MY PREMIERES ARE USUALLY IN THE LIVING ROOM WITH MY FAMILY AND OTHER TOYS.

KEY TERMS

applied behavior analysis (ABA): a type of behavior therapy that is the best evidence-based treatment for autism spectrum disorder

board certified behavior analyst (BCBA): a healthcare professional with a graduate degree who is trained to study the behavior of children and create plans to help improve or change problematic behaviors. ABA therapy should be overseen by a BCBA.

child psychiatrist: a medical doctor who completed medical school, residency training in psychiatry, and fellowship training in child psychiatry. A child psychiatrist specializes in evaluation and treatment of children with possible disorders of thinking, feeling and/or behavior.

developmental behavioral pediatrician (DBP): a medical doctor who completed medical school, residency training in general pediatrics, and fellowship training in developmental behavioral pediatrics. A DBP specializes in evaluation and treatment of children with concerns about possible developmental delay and/or concerns about difficult or atypical behaviors (such as autism spectrum disorder).

DSM-5 (Diagnostic Statistical Manual of Mental Disorders – 5th Edition): a manual (guidebook) developed by professionals in the field of psychiatry, psychology and development that outlines signs and symptoms (also known as "criteria") required for an individual to be diagnosed with a certain disorder, including autism spectrum disorder

neuropsychologist: a doctor with a PhD or PsyD who completed general training in psychology and additional training in the area of neuropsychology (how the brain processes information, including attention, language and memory)

occupational therapist: a healthcare provider with a master's degree who assesses a child's fine motor skills (for example, hand strength), self-help skills (for example, ability to feed or dress themselves), and visual skills (for example, recognizing shapes and numbers), and can provide occupational therapy to help improve these areas of a child's development

speech-language pathologist: a healthcare provider with a master's degree who assesses a child's speech and language, communication, and oral feeding skills, and can provide speech therapy to help improve these areas of a child's development

MORE INFORMATION FROM THE MEDICAL EDITOR

By Maja Z. Katusic, M.D.
Senior Associate Consultant, Department of Developmental and Behavioral Pediatrics, Mayo Clinic, Rochester, MN; Assistant Professor of Pediatrics, Mayo Clinic College of Medicine and Science

Autism spectrum disorder (ASD) is a diagnosis that describes specific difficulties with behavior, especially in the areas of social communication and restricted and repetitive behaviors. No two children who are diagnosed with autism spectrum disorder are exactly alike. However, there are overarching challenges with social communication and with restricted or repetitive behaviors that all children who are diagnosed with autism display, also known as "meeting **DSM-5** criteria" for autism, from the **Diagnostic Statistical Manual of Mental Disorders**. These difficulties include deficits in social-emotional reciprocity. For example, they may have trouble initiating or responding appropriately to social interactions or reduced sharing of interests with others.

Children with ASD also have deficits in nonverbal communication used for social interaction, including trouble with eye contact or limited facial expressions. They also exhibit deficits in developing and understanding relationships. For example, they may have trouble engaging in pretend, imaginative play without direction, or may show little interest in making friends and would prefer to play by themselves. Some examples of restricted or repetitive behaviors include lining objects up repetitively, insistence on a strict routine, or visual fascination with lights or spinning objects.

To diagnose autism spectrum disorder, a child will be evaluated by a trained professional with a specialty in evaluating children with developmental concerns. This could be a **developmental behavioral pediatrician**, a **child psychiatrist**, a **child neuropsychologist**, a **speech-language pathologist** or an **occupational therapist**. The specialist should obtain a history from the caregiver about the child's development and behavior and observe the child, and he or she may administer structured developmental testing of the child. The results of these evaluations taken together can help determine if the child indeed has a diagnosis of autism spectrum disorder and what additional therapies and interventions would be recommended.

Children who are diagnosed with autism spectrum disorder are often referred to many different types of therapies. One of the best evidence-based interventions is a behavior therapy called **applied behavior analysis**, also known as **ABA** therapy. **ABA** therapy is essentially a method to teach; it is not only used for children with ASD, but it has proven to be effective as a treatment for ASD. It helps improve behaviors a caregiver would like their child to engage in (such as requesting something using words and gestures) and decrease some more difficult behaviors (such as extreme trouble with transitions or small changes) through positive reinforcement.
ABA therapy should be supervised by a **board certified behavior analyst** (also known as a **BCBA**). **ABA** therapy should also include caregivers as an integral member of the team, so they can help with creating **ABA** therapy goals for their child and participate in extending these therapy goals into the home environment. In addition to **ABA** therapy, a child may be referred to speech or occupational therapy to help with delays in speech and language skills or delays in adaptive skills. The healthcare provider may also recommend social skills classes and parent management training or parent child interaction therapy, to help caregivers learn tools for responding to a child's various behaviors. For all these types of therapies, it is important for caregivers to be very involved in developing goals for the child and in learning how to transfer skills learned in the therapy setting into the home and community environments.

REFERENCES

American Psychiatric Association. *Diagnostic and Statistical Manual of Mental Disorders*. 5th ed. American Psychiatric Association. 2013; doi:10.1176/appi.books.9780890425596.

Hyman SL, Levy SE, Myers SM; COUNCIL ON CHILDREN WITH DISABILITIES, SECTION ON DEVELOPMENTAL AND BEHAVIORAL PEDIATRICS. Identification, Evaluation, and Management of Children With Autism Spectrum Disorder. *Pediatrics*. 2020; doi:10.1542/peds.2019-3447.

WEB RESOURCES

Autism Speaks — www.autismspeaks.org
The Autism Speaks website includes a 100 day tool kit for new diagnosis. This downloadable toolkit is created specifically for newly diagnosed families to make the best possible use of the 100 days following a child's diagnosis.

Child Mind Institute — www.childmind.org/guide/parents-guide-to-autism/
This online guide provides caregivers with a comprehensive introduction to autism.

Child Mind Institute — www.childmind.org/guide/developmental-milestones/
The Child Mind Institute also offers this guide to developmental milestones for children.

Kids Health — www.kidshealth.org/en/parents/autism-checklist-preschoolers.html?WT.
ac=ctg#catfamily
This checklist provides next steps for caregivers of a child (birth-5) diagnosed with ASD.

Centers for Disease Control and Prevention: Autism Spectrum Disorder — www.cdc.gov/
ncbddd/autism/index.html
Find additional information on ASD, including statistics, videos and related research, on this
website from the U.S. Centers for Disease Control and Prevention.

ABOUT THE MEDICAL EDITOR

Maja Z. Katusic, M.D.
Senior Associate Consultant, Department of Developmental and Behavioral Pediatrics,
Mayo Clinic, Rochester, MN; Assistant Professor of Pediatrics,
Mayo Clinic College of Medicine and Science

Dr. Katusic's clinical expertise includes comprehensive medical evaluation and management of
children from infancy through 18 years of age. The patients she works with exhibit a wide range of
developmental or behavioral concerns. She has a special clinical and research interest in autism
spectrum disorder. Dr Katusic is passionate about utilizing a patient- and family-centered
approach in creating care plans for her patients. She was honored to work with the authors on
this unique project to help improve public understanding of autism spectrum disorder.

ABOUT THE AUTHORS

Guillaume Federighi, aka **Hey Gee**, is a French and American author and illustrator. He began
his career in 1998 in Paris, France. He also spent a few decades exploring the world of street art
and graffiti in different European capitals. After moving to New York in 2008, he worked with
many companies and brands, developing a reputation in graphic design and illustration for his
distinctive style of translating complex ideas into simple and timeless visual stories.
He is also the owner and creative director of Hey Gee Studio, a full-service creative
agency based in New York City.

C. Ano is autistic and was diagnosed when he was two years old. Following his diagnosis he and
his mom spent their days playing and attending his early intervention sessions with different
types of therapists, including an occupational therapist, a speech therapist and a floor time
therapist. Being present and engaged with the care team was important to his mom to ensure
that each member of the therapy team was the right fit for C. Ano, working toward goals that
were supportive of his growth and not restrictive. C. Ano is 13 years old now. He loves drawing
and being creative and has started his own comic book series. His favorite author/illustrators are
Jeff Kinney and Dav Pilkey. He also enjoys creating original movies with his toys and has created a
one-act play. C. Ano is a talented public speaker and aspires to be a movie director or an author/
illustrator. He lives in Minnesota with his parents, younger brother and two dogs.

ABOUT FONDATION IPSEN BOOKLAB

Fondation Ipsen improves the lives of millions of people around the world by rethinking scientific communication. The truthful transmission of science to the public is complex because scientific information is often technical and there is a lot of inaccurate information. In 2018, Fondation Ipsen established BookLab to address this need. BookLab books come about through collaboration between scientists, doctors, artists, authors, and children. In paper and electronic formats, and in several languages, BookLab delivers books across more than 50 countries for people of all ages and cultures. Fondation Ipsen BookLab's publications are free of charge to schools, libraries and people living in precarious situations. Join us! Access and share our books by visiting: www.fondation-ipsen.org.

ABOUT MAYO CLINIC PRESS

Launched in 2019, Mayo Clinic Press shines a light on the most fascinating stories in medicine and empowers individuals with the knowledge to build healthier, happier lives. From the award-winning *Mayo Clinic Health Letter* to books and media covering the scope of human health and wellness, Mayo Clinic Press publications provide readers with reliable and trusted content by some of the world's leading health care professionals. Proceeds benefit important medical research and education at Mayo Clinic. For more information about Mayo Clinic Press, visit mcpress.mayoclinic.org.

ABOUT THE COLLABORATION

The My Life Beyond series was developed in partnership between Fondation Ipsen's BookLab and Mayo Clinic, which has provided world-class medical education for more than 150 years. This collaboration aims to provide trustworthy, impactful resources for understanding childhood diseases and other problems that can affect children's well-being.

The series offers readers a holistic perspective of children's lives with — and beyond — their medical challenges. In creating these books, young people who have been Mayo Clinic patients worked together with author-illustrator Hey Gee, sharing their personal experiences. The resulting fictionalized stories authentically bring to life the patients' emotions and their inspiring responses to challenging circumstances. In addition, Mayo Clinic physicians contributed the latest medical expertise on each topic so that these stories can best help other patients, families and caregivers understand how children perceive and work through their own challenges.

Text: Hey Gee and C. Ano
Illustrations: Hey Gee

Medical editor: Maja Z. Katusic, M.D., Senior Associate Consultant, Department of Developmental and Behavioral Pediatrics, Mayo Clinic, Rochester, MN; Assistant Professor of Pediatrics, Mayo Clinic College of Medicine and Science

Managing editor: Anna Cavallo, Health Education and Content Services/Mayo Clinic Press, Mayo Clinic, Rochester, MN
Project manager: Kim Chandler, Department of Education, Mayo Clinic, Rochester, MN
Manager of publications: Céline Colombier-Maffre, Fondation Ipsen, Paris, France
President: James A. Levine, M.D., Ph.D., Professor, Fondation Ipsen, Paris, France

MAYO CLINIC PRESS
200 First St. SW
Rochester, MN 55905
mcpress.mayoclinic.org

The information in this book is true and complete to the best of our knowledge. This book is intended only as an informative guide for those wishing to learn more about health issues. It is not intended to replace, countermand or conflict with advice given to you by your own physician. The ultimate decision concerning your care should be made between you and your doctor. Information in this book is offered with no guarantees. The author and publisher disclaim all liability in connection with the use of this book.

For bulk sales to employers, member groups and health-related companies, contact Mayo Clinic, 200 First St. SW, Rochester, MN 55905, or send an email to SpecialSalesMayoBooks@mayo.edu.

Proceeds from the sale of every book benefit important medical research and education at Mayo Clinic.

ISBN 978-1-893005-77-8

Library of Congress Control Number 2021943745

Printed in the United States of America